MOBSTERS
I HAVE KNOWN & LOVED

———❖———

FRANCES McKEE

Wasteland Press
Shelbyville, KY USA
www.wastelandpress.net

Mobsters I Have Known & Loved
by Frances McKee

Copyright © 2009 Frances McKee
ALL RIGHTS RESERVED

First Printing—November 2009
ISBN: 978-1-60047-376-0

*Front cover photo of Anthony "Little Pussy" Russo,
courtesy of www.phillymobspot.com*

Printed in the U.S.A.

To "Little Pussy"—

May God bless you wherever you are…

Acknowledgement

I wish to thank from the bottom of my heart my editor, agent, and very dear friend, Susan Giffin. Without her patience, forbearance, knowledge, and great sense of humor, this book would never have come into being. I do not know what I would have done without her.

God bless you, Susan, every day that you live.

Contents

Prologue

In June of 1962, a restaurant opened in Long Branch, New Jersey—the Surf Lounge. On the surface, there was not too much difference in this restaurant, compared to others. The food was Italian, the kind you got in your grandmother's kitchen. The décor was lovely, all silver and blue with touches of black. The service? Unique. That was not the only difference, however, as you will see.

At the time, my husband was in the United States Marine Corps. He was to go overseas, but I could not accompany him, so I went home to New Jersey to be with my family. Times being what they were, I had to go to work. My first job was with the Landmark Hotel, and then I went to the Surf intending to stay only fourteen months; I stayed fourteen *years*. But this is not the story of my life, only a small part of it, but these were my "salad days."

The Surf, at that time, was owned by James "Skippy" Faye and Pat Simonetti. Skippy, a plumber and self-made millionaire, who was handsome as a movie star, was a kind, witty man, a true gentleman. God bless you, Skippy, wherever you are.

Pat Simonetti, his partner, was born to own a restaurant. He greeted his customers as if they were entering his own home. He loved "his people," the business, and life in general. He made all of his customers feel as if he was waiting all night just for them to come in. The funny thing is he was. He loved entertaining his friends. He sang with the band. Now, don't get me wrong; he was no threat to Frank Sinatra, but he could "put over a song." He was a compassionate man with a dynamite personality. He was also the son-in-law of Vito "Don Vito" Genovese, the reputed "vice lord of America." Because of this, the Surf had the reputation of being a "Mob hangout." Yet Pat was no more a member of organized crime than I was.

Mr. Genovese was, at the time, serving a prison term and "for respect of Vito," many reputed mobsters patronized the restaurant. Another contributing factor to the Surf's undeserved reputation was the fact that the property once belonged to Anthony "Little Pussy" Russo, the "gambling boss of Monmouth County." Pussy sold the property to Pat and Skippy. It was a charming old boarding house half a block from the ocean. They turned it into a restaurant, yet many people to this day believe that Pussy was the owner of the Surf.

It was a fun place; all the owners, waitresses, bartenders, chefs, janitor, as well as the customers, are characters. One of the "wise guys" described it very well. "This is the kind of a place that if I forget what day it is, I have only to look at the faces at the table and say, 'Oh, it's Tuesday.'"

The "crew" loved one another. We even spent our days off together. Maybe we hold a place in the *Guinness Book of World Records*. The same crew was there from the day the Surf opened until the day Pat sold it. No one quit; no one was fired. Waiters, waitresses, and bartenders are like "whores;" they don't stay in the same place too long. Here, only three people left. One girl died. The original chef got divorced and moved to another state, and one bartender opened his own place.

There was no petty jealousy or backstabbing. We helped one another; we even lied for one another. It was a sort of magic, in that all the right people were in the same place at the right time. Pat, Skippy, and the customers treated us like "family." Pat sold the place in 1969, but till today, he calls us "his girls."

I stayed with the new owners until 1976. Joe and Marion Agnellino ran the place on more efficient lines, and many of the old customers stayed also. Joe was a lion of a man. He was the most honorable person I ever knew. He was a quiet man, with a dry sense of humor, and he was very good to his crew. All loved and respected him, but with Pat gone, the atmosphere did change. Marion was more of a "mixer." She had a lovely way about her; she indulged her customers. In a lot of way, she was much easier to talk to than Joe.

Joe is gone now, and I bless his memory.

Well, I started to write this in 1990. A lot of water has run under the bridge. Time has a funny way of distorting memory, and I have to reach back to 1961 to tell these stories. For those "still left" and who also remember, I beg indulgence if I am not one hundred percent accurate.

I really should include all of the wonderful people who are a part of the Surf's history, but that would fill ten books. To include all of the funny things that happen here would fill ten libraries.

One mobster, Anthony "Little Pussy" Russo, stands out among all the mobsters I have known and loved. He appears in almost every chapter of this book, because he touched many lives at the Surf, but I'm saving some of his best stories for last. It's only fitting I would do so. After all, you don't want to serve the main course before you take time to enjoy the antipasto and such leading up to it.

Besides, I had promised him that one day I would write this book. His only wish was that I write it "after I'm dead."

Well, Pussy, you've been dead thirty-one years now. For me, you never died, so here goes...

—Frances Esposito McKee

Chapter 1

The Landmark Hotel & Lounge

May 1961: Joe, my husband, was scheduled to be shipped out to Okinawa for twenty-two months. My mother did not want the kids and me to be alone in San Francisco, our last duty station, so we returned to New Jersey. Joseph, my son, was five and Nora, my daughter, was two-and-a-half. I was twenty-eight. I was happy to be home, but I missed my husband and all the great friends I left behind in California.

Before my marriage, I had served for four years in the United States Marine Corps. My principal accomplishment while in the service was finishing college. I taught history for one year and then got married. In San Francisco, I worked for the Pacific Institute for the Blind.

Now, back home in New Jersey, I knew I had to go to work, but I hated to leave the kids, so I looked for a night job. I felt that this way the kids would not be deprived of both mother and father. Mom was willing to care for them, and heaven knows she was much more capable than I was. Still, I felt guilty not spending all of my time with them.

I was collecting unemployment insurance when Lisa, an old school chum, called me about a job. A beautiful young girl with four daughters, she was working nights so her husband Bob could get his degree in engineering. He was an extremely jealous man, and he was giving Lisa a bad time.

As she explained to me, "My job at the Landmark is the nicest job I have ever had. I earn more money here in two days than I did in any other job working five days." She was very upset. She worked in the cocktail lounge at the hotel, but her husband wanted her to cut back on her hours, not because of the money, but because he was jealous.

"My boss told me that if I could get someone to work my Fridays and Saturdays," Lisa said, "I could work Sundays and Mondays, and they would make up the difference in tips out of their own pockets."

Lisa asked me to work the weekends for her. I told her I would be very happy to help out, but that I knew nothing about serving cocktails. She assured me that it was alright with "them." She had explained to them that I was a school teacher.

I have to admit I was intrigued. What kind of employers would make up money out of their own pockets for a worker? I was to find out very soon. Lisa asked if it was alright for her boss to call me. The next night he did.

Mom answered the phone. "Tootsie, there's a man asking for you. I can't understand a word he is saying." There was nothing unusual about that. Mom had trouble understanding a lot of people.

What followed was the strangest phone call I ever got. "Is dis Frances?"

"Yes," I said, "this is Frances. Who is this?"

"I'm Vitamins, Lisa's boss. I understand youse are gonna work for Lisa."

I explained to him that I had no experience, that what I knew about cocktails he could put in a cocktail glass.

"Dat's alright; you're not stupid, are you?"

I was taken aback somewhat, but I found myself liking the person on the other end of the line.

"Look, you'll learn, besides you don't have to know nothin', the bartender has to know everything. You just be a parrot."

I told him that I would like to come on a night when they were not busy. I would come on my own time, I said, and in this way, I would see if I liked them and they liked me.

"Okay, kid. By the way, how old are you?" he asked.

"Twenty-eight."

"Fifty-eight!" he gasped.

"Mr. Vitamins, if I was fifty-eight, I would hang up the phone."

This amused him. We agreed that I would come in on a Thursday to "try it out."

The Landmark was an old hotel with a diner-type restaurant in the front and a cocktail lounge in the back. Instead of regular tables and chairs, it had a bar and living room furniture—sofas and chairs with deep cushions. It was a cozy-looking place, decorated in soft, muted colors of grey, beige, and gold. A year later, a club in New

York opened and enjoyed great success along the same lines. It was called "The Living Room." Who knows, they may have copied Jimmy Vitamins' idea.

I was very nervous about going to work at the Landmark, because, as I said, I knew nothing about waitress work. I read up on it and found that in the formal dining room, your employer was always referred to as "Mr." This applied to the maitre d' and all other males of importance.

I dressed with care that night, determined to make a good impression. I did not want to let Lisa down. I had no way of knowing at that time that "they" were prepared to love me, come hell or high water. You see, in the code of the underworld, I was a "stand-up friend." The Mob respected education, and not only was I a school teacher, but I was also willing to lower myself to help a friend.

Jimmy Vitamins greeted me at the door. He was about five foot ten, well built with black wavy hair and large black eyes. I remember thinking, this man looks like a prize fighter. His face was pushed in. He reminded me of a friendly bulldog, if you can imagine a bulldog with an Italian face, that is. He was beautifully dressed, and his smile lit up his face.

He introduced me to the bartender, Johnny Rao, and then left to attend to some business. Johnny, a great big Teddy bear of a man, put me at ease. He explained the system of serving cocktails. I was given a twenty-five dollar "bank." I would take the orders and come to the bar. When Johnny gave me the drinks, I would pay him for them, and then I would collect the money from my customers. He went on to explain that at the end of the night, I would give him back the twenty-five dollar bank, and the rest of the money in my pocket was my tips.

It was a slow night, being a Thursday in January. Long Branch is a summer resort, so all business slowed down in the winter. I was introduced to the boss, Tommy Rocco. Tommy insisted I eat something, as it would probably be a long night. I told him I loved ziti. To my surprise, he not only cooked it himself, but he also served it to me. He was a kind, gentle man with the bluest eyes I had ever seen. Later, I nicknamed him "Tommy Blue Eyes." The name has stuck till today.

Around 10 p.m., the customers started arriving. In my nervousness, I did not notice that they were all men. They came in twos, threes, sixes, and some singles. I panicked. The orders were coming in fast and furiously. I didn't know a martini from a zombie. Three quarters of the poor guys got the wrong drinks, wrong change, etc. Not one single complaint. The only time they corrected me on their change was when I was cheating myself! They behaved like princes of the Blood Royal.

One kind man forced me to "sit down and take a break; no one will order for at least fifteen minutes." Months later, I found out that that "kind man" was wanted in six states.

After what seemed like months, the bar emptied. The last customers to arrive were six men. The oldest, a white-haired man, was accompanied by five young men, who treated him with reverence. I thought to myself; look at that nice Italian man with his dutiful sons. Well, the "nice Italian man" turned out to be a Jewish fence (one who buys and sells stolen goods), and the five young men? His underlings.

Johnny assured me I was doing a good job. I knew better. But where was Vitamins? I figured he could not stand the disaster I had made of the bar, so I turned in my bank and literally flew out of the place.

Mom was waiting up for me when I arrived. "How did it go?" she asked.

I gave her all the gory details. As I was talking to her, I emptied my pockets, all one hundred and seven dollars! This, in 1961! Why, some of our family didn't earn that much in a week.

"Where did you get all that money?" she screamed.

"My tips," I whispered.

"What kind of job do you have?"

Well, I really could not answer, because I was wondering that myself. Then I told her, "You know, Mom, those people did not speak English too well, but they had the patience of saints. I think they felt sorry for me, so they tipped me lavishly."

It would be some time before I realized that I had unknowingly cheated them of their change, and they were too polite to tell me.

The next afternoon, Vitamins called me. He sounded so worried. "Frances, what happened? Did anyone insult you?"

I told him that, on the contrary, they could not have treated me better if I was the Queen of England.

"Oh, you left so fast. I was worried. Well, will you come back next Friday?"

"You want me back?" I screamed.

"Of course, we want you back. Look, no one was born knowing how to serve cocktails. You'll learn, and I swear on my mother, you will not be alone. Lisa will help you till you know what you're doing."

By now, I was almost in tears.

"Look, kid, you got class. Nobody ever answered the phone here so polite-like. You give the place class."

So, back I went.

After two nights (with Lisa's help), I was ready to fly solo. I looked forward to going to work. Mr. Rocco treated me with kid gloves. His wife Julia behaved like my mother, and his daughter Tootsie was a jewel. How she laughed when I told her my nickname was also Tootsie. We both hated the name, and I had almost managed to forget about it.

Two weeks passed. One night, Vitamins was more nervous than ever. The man was shambling wreck. By the way, that was how he had earned his nickname. He swallowed pills like candy— pills to go to sleep, pills to wake up, pills to calm down. So how come Vitamins? One of the local wits said he reminded one and all of "Vitamin Flintheart," a character in the Dick Tracy comic strip, henceforth the name.

Anyway, this particular night, he behaved as if he was going to the electric chair the next day. "Frances, I'm waiting for Louie Ross. When he comes, we have to go pick up the boss at the airport."

I was very puzzled. The boss? Mr. Rocco was in the kitchen. What boss was he talking about?

"Now, don't be nervous, kid. Just answer the phone and take any messages. Anybody bothers you, hang up."

I could not understand why Mr. Vitamins had so much patience with me. He had hired and fired fourteen crews until I appeared on the scene. Every week there had been an ad in the local newspapers, "WANTED: Waitress. Apply Landmark Lounge." He fired people at the drop of a hat.

Louis Ross finally arrived. He was greeted with shouts of "Goddamn you, Louie, we are late. Do you want him to cut off my cujones?"

The undaunted Louie just smiled. There was no hurrying him. He had only two gears: slow and reverse. Off they went, and I sat down for a cup of coffee.

A little later, the phone rang. "Good evening, Landmark Lounge," I said.

Stone silence on the other end.

"Hello, hello, may I help you?"

A growling sound came over the line, "V-i-t-a-m-i-n-s."

"I'm so sorry, Mr. Vitamins is not here. How may I help you?"

I hear soft laughter on the other end. You see, they were not used to hearing a cultured voice in the Landmark, of all places. "May I ask who's calling?"

"Pussy," was the reply.

I was filled with rage! I banged the receiver so hard I almost broke the phone. No one paid the slightest attention.

Shortly after that, a man came in and sat at the only table in the room. It was in the darkest corner by the bar.

"Good evening, sir, what can I get for you?"

The man studied me as if I were a rare specimen. He was slightly balding with a pleasant face, a round cherry tomato nose, and a magnificent set of teeth. "Lemon juice."

"Yes, sir, and what would you like with it?" I was trying not to show that I was miffed.

"Lemon juice," he drawled.

"Yes, sir, would you like that straight, on the rocks or intravenous?" I snapped.

He just smiled.

I stormed up to the bar. Johnny could see that I was annoyed. He was trying to see who was at the corner table. In tones dripping with sarcasm, I asked for the lemon juice. He reacted as if I had shot him. Handing me the glass, he whispered, "Oh, God, Frances, please be nice."

Without uttering a word, I set the little man's drink down. I busied myself elsewhere, ignoring him completely.

I was pouring a cup of coffee, when Vitamins rushed passed me and almost knocked me down. "Jesus Christ, Louie! Where is Pussy? How could you have missed him?" he kept moaning over and over.

The smiling Louie couldn't have cared less. Nevertheless, he tried to placate him. "You know Pussy; he probably changed his mind and took a cab."

Vitamins was not convinced. Turning to me, he asked if anyone had called for him. In icy tones, I informed him that there had been only one call.

"Who was it?"

"I don't know."

"Well, what did he say?"

"I wouldn't care to repeat it, Mr. Vitamins."

He tried to hide his smile.

"It's okay, Frances. You can tell me."

"Mr. Vitamins, I was very polite. I asked who was calling. Do you know what he called me? Pussy! That's what he said to me."

All the color drained from his face. "What did you do?" he whispered.

"I hung up!"

I thought he was going to faint. "My God, Louie, she hung up."

Before I could reply, an ominous voice came from the corner table. "V-i-t-a-m-i-n-s."

Rushing to the table, wringing his hands, he pleaded, "Boss, I'm sorry. She's a new girl…"

I could not hear the rest of the conversation, and then the little man got up to leave.

"Stop him," I shouted.

Physically restraining me, Vitamins assured me it was alright.

"It's not alright. He didn't pay me. My bank will be short," I yelled.

Poor Vitamins. He was almost in tears. "I'll pay you."

I stopped dead in my tracks. He would pay me? This guy tossed around nickels like they were manhole covers. Who was that man? In two months, I would find out.

Vitamins, accompanied by the little man, and Louie left. Happy as a lark, Vitamins returned and handed me a twenty-dollar bill.

"What's that?" I asked suspiciously.

"Your tip from the Boss."

Lord, would these wonders ever cease? I told Vitamins that the whole thing was ridiculous. "I served the man only one drink."

"I know," smiled Vitamins. "He said that was the best laugh he had in twenty years, one dollar per year."

Well, all's well that ends well.

A week later, the little man came in again. Vitamins called me over to introduce him. "Frances, come meet the Boss."

Here we go again, gang. Boss of what? "How do you do, sir. What do I call you?"

"Pussy," he replied, dead-panned.

Well, I was not about to let this uncouth savage rattle me. In the sweetest tones I could muster, I asked, "Yes, sir, what is your last name?"

He studied me for a moment. Now there was a twinkle in his eye. "Pussy," he replied.

Touché, bastard! If that's the way you want it, that's the way you'll get it. I continued to call him "Mr. Pussy" till we all left the Landmark.

For a while, I was under the impression that Vitamins was working two jobs. He was the manager of the Landmark, and he also worked in some capacity or another for Pussy. It was Tommy Rocco who enlightened me. Jimmy was Pussy's aide de camp. High class errand boy, if you will. It seems that he was always in trouble, so Mr. Rocco was doing Pussy a favor. Running the lounge was a punishment; now Vitamins had to work for a living. He took out his frustration on the crew. There were times when he could be a living doll. He was witty, but most of the time he was a real mutt.

When Vitamins was broke, he behaved like a human being, but when he had a few dollars in his pocket he turned into a savage. It was now that I found out that poor Lisa was in love with him. You would think that having a girl as beautiful and kind as she was would have humbled him a bit, but, no, he was as proud as Lucifer. I'm afraid he treated Lisa rather shabbily and, to top it all off, he cheated on her. She got even in the end. Unwittingly I was the one who helped her.

Chapter 2

Boston Butchie

"Boston Butchie" was Vitamins' chum. He was, in fact, one of the few people who really liked Vitamins. Butch was a good-looking version of Neville Brand, the actor. Like most of the others, he was a fashion plate. How he and Vitamins became best friends, I do not know, because Vitamins grew up in Newark, and Butch in Boston.

Butch was always pleasant to me, but we weren't close like some of the other mobsters who became my "fiancés."

I came to work one night and found Lisa waiting for me. She was distressed and crying. She told me how rotten Vitamins was, how he treated her like dirt, how he was a cheat, a liar, etc. Trying to calm her down, I gave her a brandy, and it seemed to help.

"If only I could get back at that son-of-a-bitch," she said. "I would feel 100 percent better."

I advised her to try and forget him. She was too good for him. For God's sake, she could have had any one of them, even Pussy. (She thought I was telling her to use the old jealousy routine.) She really wanted to get back at him and getting him jealous wouldn't be enough. Figuring that she just wanted to blow off steam and would not listen to me anyway, I told her, "If you really want to get even with him, sleep with his best friend."

How could I know she would do just that? Unbeknownst to me, it was the beginning of Lisa and Boston Butchie. It was also the beginning of the end for Vitamins and me.

Butch liked Lisa. He was appalled by Vitamins' treatment of her. I'm sure that he was under the impression that Vitamins didn't really care for her. So, you got it; she started going out with Butch.

Meanwhile, Vitamins was starting to treat me like dirt, and I couldn't understand it. He called me "stool pigeon, rat, Mother Superior." You name it.

One night I confronted him. "Why are you doing this to me?"

He snarled back, "You listen to my phone conversations and report back to Lisa."

This was not so, and I told him I was not guilty.

"Yeah, well how did Lisa know that I was at the Copa last night?"

I was tempted to hit him. "How should I know? I didn't know you were the Copa last night, so how could I have told her?"

From time to time, Butch would ask me why Vitamins hated me so much. I could not tell him that it was because of Lisa, since, by then, I knew that he too was seeing her. I thought that discretion was the better part of valor.

Things came to a head one night in the parking lot. As I was getting out of my car, Vitamins was driving into the lot with Butch. He made as if to run over me, missing me by inches. I called him a "goddamned creep" and picked up a rock to throw at his car.

Butch was furious with Vitamins. "What the hell did you do that for? That girl is good to everybody," he bellowed.

Vitamins told him I was a stool pigeon. "She's always on the Erie, and she tells Lisa where I'm going and what I'm doing."

How could I say anything with Butch standing there? I just went inside and got ready for my shift.

Later that night, Vitamins left, and Butch came over to ask me what it was all about. I told him the whole story and begged him not to tell Vitamins. Mutt that he was I didn't want him to be hurt. Even though I had just been kidding when I told Lisa to cheat on him with his best friend if she wanted to get back at him, I felt guilty.

I expected Butch to laugh about the whole thing, but he was very upset. He told me that he was the guilty one. He had no idea that the Lisa and Vitamins really cared for each other, and that he was the one telling Lisa where Vitamins was going. He suggested we come clean. "Why should you take the rap?"

I pointed out to him that I meant nothing to Vitamins, but that he did, so why break up a friendship? I won Butch's undying admiration that night, and he went out of his way to be doubly kind to me.

Still, Vitamins couldn't understand how she came by all this information. Never once did he suspect Butchie.

When Vitamins was particularly nasty to me, Butch would reprimand him. "You are wrong," he would say. "This is the best fuckin' broad in Long Branch. Let's tell him, Frannie." I would never agree. I know Vitamins was puzzled, but he had too much pride to ask what it was all about. So life went on.

Finally, it got so bad that one night, I just grabbed my purse and left in the middle of my shift.

The next day, Julia, Tommy Rocco's wife, called and asked why I had left so suddenly.

"I'm sorry, Julia, I love you and your family, but I can't take it any longer. I wouldn't take that from my husband or my father, and I'm not taking it from that creep. I am not coming back."

I felt so bad about the whole thing, so I decided to visit my Aunt Sophie for a couple of days in the Bronx. No one in our family was like Aunt Sophie. She was my soul mate. I could tell her anything. We talked about the Landmark "incident," and she agreed with me that I had done the right thing.

I didn't have the heart to tell Vitamins about Butchie and Lisa; they, in turn, did not know of Vitamins' abusing me. I was between a rock and a hard place.

When I returned to New Jersey, my mother was annoyed with me because the phone had been "ringing off the wall." Tommy, Lisa, Louie, Johnny Rao, and God-knows-who-else had called. From Vitamins? Silence!

We had just finished eating when Tommy Rocco called again. He was very upset, and he told me that if I came back, he would throw Vitamins out on his ear. I didn't want that; besides, I felt guilty. Then he told me of Pussy's wrath. It seems that when Pussy returned from Florida the following night, he had asked Vitamins, "Where's the Sicilian?" Stammering, Vitamins told him that I had quit.

"If that kid quit, you were at your fucking worst. You get her back here if you want to be around this Easter."

Poor Tommy, he was really shook up. He assured me that Pussy would really hurt Vitamins if I didn't return. I explained to Tommy that if I came back, Vitamins himself would have to call me. It wasn't pride on my part, but if I came back without him asking me to, he would go on to make my life miserable. On that note, we left off.

The following morning, Vitamins called. He did not apologize (I didn't expect him to), but the call was enough (or so I thought). Anyway, I returned to the Landmark.

For the next two months, life went on as usual. Vitamins treated me coldly, speaking only when necessary, but if looks could kill, I would have died before my twenty-ninth birthday. The rest of the guys treated me even better than before. Pussy loved and valued me. I was a "woman of respect." The more they loved me, the more Vitamins hated me.

Our little love triangle deception finally came out in the wash, only this wash was a tray of drinks, not water. Butch told the regular customers that I was a stand-up broad. All the guys knew the story of the eternal triangle. Instead of sympathizing with

Vitamins, they were on my side. Those devils were amused by the whole thing. Pat Simonetti told one and all, "She called Vitamins a creep." Ray Crow, one of the regulars, quipped, "Who will win, Beauty or the Beast?" The tension mounted, and then one night it ended.

I was trying to get past Vitamins with a full tray of drinks. He deliberately blocked my way. There I was holding the tray over my head (and his), trying to squeeze past him.

"I'll give you five hundred dollars if you drop those drinks on his head," yelled Andy Gerard, another regular.

I swear on my immortal soul it was an accident. The heel of my shoe got caught in a tear in the rug, down came the drinks, fruit and all, all over his three-hundred-dollar suit. There was nothing he could do. Pussy, Andy, and Butch formed a protective ring around me. Vitamins was not about to take them on, so he pretended to laugh along with them.

I kept repeating over and over again, "It was an accident, I swear."

Andy pretended to write me a check, and Vitamins swore to Butch that he would get even if it took him the rest of his life. This was too much for Butch. Grabbing Vitamins in a corner, Butch told him, "Leave her alone. She didn't tell Lisa. I did, but I did it innocently." He went on to tell him that he'd been seeing Lisa all along.

Vitamins did not believe him. He thought he was trying to shield me. "You don't have Lisa's private phone number."

Butch showed him the number in his little black book. Poor Vitamins looked so hurt. I would have given anything to spare him that. Butch went on to tell him the story from A to Z, grabbing both of his hands.

"You knew all along and you didn't tell me?" Vitamins gently asked me.

"I couldn't tell you that," I sobbed.

"You took all that abuse undeservedly," he said. "I am so sorry. Please forgive me."

The contest was over, but nobody won. We all lost something. Only one thing was gained. Vitamins and I became friends again. Shortly after that, he went to New Orleans, where he died at the age of forty-two from cirrhosis of the liver. I thank God we mended our fences before it was too late.

One Sunday afternoon, I took my children to Asbury Park. In the arcade, I ran into Butch and his girl, Dotty. They were at one of those rip-off stands where you had to knock down three bowling pins to win a prize.

"Come on, Frannie," he greeted us. "You and me, we'll knock down these pins and win a prize."

I told him it would take not only the accuracy of Sergeant York, but you would also have to have the strength of Charles Atlas to accomplish that. The damned things were weighted down with lead. He and I, combined, weighed less than three hundred pounds.

Besides, I had promised to take my kids on the rides. My three-year-old Nora started to cry. She fell in love with this life-sized stuffed St. Bernard, one of the prizes. She piteously begged us to win it for her. So, for a good hour, we tried our best. The damned kid would not stop crying. She wanted that dog.

With all the patience of a saint, Butch promised that she would have the dog, even if he had to buy it. He asked the young man running the game, "How much for the dog, kid?"

The boy told him he could not sell it to him. It was against the rules.

Butch offered him fifty dollars for the dog (three times the price of the stuffed animal back then) and pushed the money into his hand. "Look, kid, just tell your boss somebody won it. You keep the fifty dollars."

To his annoyance, the kid still refused. Now, we saw a different Butch; no more Mr. Nice Guy. Grabbing the kid by the lapels, looking like a mad dog, he shouted, "KID, GIVE ME THE FUCKIN' DOG!"

The boy looked like he would faint. He handed Butch the dog and refused to take the money.

Dotty called Butch a big bully and stormed off. Poor Butch, he would not have hurt the boy. He apologized to the kid and gave him a hundred dollars. Now, everybody was happy.

P.S. We still have the St. Bernard.

Butch and I became closer friends. There as much bantering back and forth between us. I teased him about being a dandy, and he accused me of wearing falsies. How I enjoyed that man! He could say the most outrageous things with a straight face.

One night, I was admiring his shirt. The pocket was monogrammed with F.M. I accused him of stealing someone's clothes.

"It's my shirt," he barked.

"Oh, so your real name is Frank?" I quipped.

He denied it.

"Does the F stand for Filippe?" I asked.

"No."

"Does it stand for Felice?"

"No, it does not."

"What the hell does it stand for?"

Without moving a muscle, he replied, "It stands for Fuck, but keep it under your hat."

For ten years, I did just that. In Chapter 20, I reveal why I broke the promise.

Chapter 3

Transitions

How I dreaded leaving the Landmark! I didn't know, of course, that I would be going to the Surf. To this day, I do not know who wanted me there. I thought I would be leaving all the wonderful friends I had made at the Landmark.

When I finally heard more about the Surf, I panicked. This was to be a large place with a separate bar and restaurant. I knew nothing about serving food. Pat Simonetti reassured me that I would the head waitress in the lounge. This terrified me.

As it turned out, there were four waitresses in the bar (I had three girls under me), and five in the dining room. This challenge, however, was two months away.

One dull night, Louie the "Killer" brought in an old friend, Jerry Chokes. This man had eyeglasses as thick as Coca-Cola bottles. He was very friendly, and he kept buying rounds of drinks for his friends. I noticed a beautiful jade ring on his finger. I told him how valuable it was. He seemed surprised and told me it was a gift from a friend who was not moneyed.

I told him that since the Iron Curtain went around China, the value of jade was ten times higher. He offered me the ring, and I refused, of course. Now, I was impressed by the man's generosity. He offered to buy me dinner, saying he had a date and could not eat with "us."

That night we were having scungille (conch), one of my favorite dishes. I told him I loved scungille more than I loved my husband. Chokes promptly nicknamed me "Scungille." That night, I fell in love with that homely man. He was so good-natured.

Louie told me that his friends were always playing jokes on Chokes, and he took it all with good grace. I was to see first-hand one of their pranks.

Chokes said he was late for his date and had to leave. Two minutes later, he rushed back into the bar, screaming "They stole my car!"

I felt so bad for him; I offered him my car.

He reacted like a person hit by a bolt of lightning. "Miss, you can't really mean to lend me your car!"

Of course, I meant it. I was sure he would not steal it.

"Your car is only three weeks old, and you want to lend it to me?"

What the hell was all the fuss about? I knew I could get a ride home. At that point, that handsome devil, Billy Boy, "found" Chokes' car. They had hid it as a joke. When they saw that I meant to give him my three-week-old Corvette, they panicked. You see, Chokes was not only half-blind, he was the worst driver in the world. To put it in Louie's words, "This is the kind of a nut who drives down the street and takes fenders off cars parked on both sides."

How in the world could I have known this? No wonder the man thought I was the sweetest thing on earth. He insisted I take his jade ring. I told him I did not like the ring.

"Well, what do you like? You name it. You got it."

I told him I only like scungille, so he promised that before the week was out I would have a case of scungille sent to my house. True to his word, a week later TWO cases came. One was canned scungille; the other, a wooden crate as large as a casket with fresh conch in the shell. This was a very expensive proposition, as canned conch was over two dollars a can back then, and the fresh was double that price.

My mother was very suspicious of me for a long time. She would not believe that a perfect stranger would go to the trouble and expense that he had to thank someone for a kindness. The world being what it was (and still is); very few people keep their promises, even silly ones.

For the next two months, I worked seven nights a week. This was fine with me; my mother was livid, however. She was to be further enraged because of another incident involving my little red Corvette.

It delighted me to no end to watch Pussy and his entourage entering the place. If Pussy was smiling, everybody was smiling.

He kept his sunglasses in his breast pocket, with one temple hanging out. Every one of them did the same thing with their sunglasses. How I teased Pussy about that! How I loved him!

Well, this night, he came in cursing, "I want to strangle him in the coffin for what he done to me, that fat bastard." He muttered this over and over, and the others were muttering, too, but I could not make out what they were saying. I was alarmed, because Pussy had a very bad blood pressure problem, and his face was as red as a tomato.

"Please, boss, calm down. Let me get you some black coffee," I begged.

"Ah, Frances," he replied, "I should've taken singing lessons. If this keeps up, I will."

We all chuckled at his little joke. He couldn't carry a tune in a bucket.

While serving the coffee, I asked him what was troubling him.

"Jackson dropped dead at thirty-eight years old," he said. "What a mess he left me. To top it all off, I have to go to the wake, and the goddamned FBI will be watching all the cars."

I did not know Jackson, nor did I know what he died of. I certainly wasn't going to ask about the "mess," either. Still I wanted to comfort him. I hit on a brilliant idea. "Boss," I said, "take my car. I have California plates on it. Let them figure that out."

His face lit up with that radiant smile of his, but he shook his head. "No, I can't take your car to the funeral, honey. It's red."

I pointed out to him that he was going to the wake, not the funeral, and the car could be parked in the parking lot. He thought it over for a while and then agreed to switch cars. That was the end of it...

A few weeks later, two FBI agents showed up at my mother's house. They wanted to question me about Eddie Gurrazio. I informed them that I did not know anyone by that name (to this day, I am not sure about it). They kept insisting—politely, of course—that I was lying.

I, in turn, insisted that my parents had lived there for only five years, and I was away for those years with my husband who was in the military. Consequently, I knew very few people in New Jersey.

The agents came up with the trump card. "You attended this man's wake," they smirked.

At this point, I was getting annoyed, and my mother was close to fainting. Then I remembered that Pussy had taken my car to a wake for a man named "Jackson."

"Oh," I said, "you mean Jackson. I never met the man."

Of course, they wanted to know how I knew this Eddie Gurrazio's alias. I told them that the man's mistress was going to his wake, and her car broke down, so I lent her mine.

"How come you know the man's mistress, but you don't know the man?" they asked.

I told him she was a customer and now they were suspicious indeed. Later I found that the man did have a mistress, but she lived in Memphis, Tennessee. I had just made up the story, albeit accurate, on the spot.

The weeks flew by; they always do when you're happy. I got to know some of the guys and every week I grew fonder of Pussy. He was such an "up," always joking, playing little pranks, like stealing my tips and then giving them back to me at the end of the night. He loved to hear me say, "Keep the damned money. You need it more than I do."

If Pussy was in a bad mood—which put Vitamins at his absolute worst—I would borrow one of my husband's expressions and say, "How do you get a transfer out of this chicken shit outfit?"

He would laugh and say, "Don't worry. We're going."

They were getting ready to open the Surf in June, and that's what he meant.

There was no let-up from my mother. "Quit that place," she would tell me. "How can you bring this disgrace upon us?" And on and on and on.

I would tell her that in June I would be gone from there. What I didn't tell her was that I was going to a place with the same people (thank God). Perhaps I was wrong, but I found it easier to survive with my mother when I told her half-truths or out-and-out lies. Telling the truth was very painful for me.

Chapter 4

The Surf Lounge

The Surf's co-owners were Skippy Faye and Pat Simonetti. Skippy Faye wanted the cocktail waitresses to be glamorous, to have uniforms that were completely different from those worn in other restaurants. He thought something in black and gold (to complement the décor of the lounge) would be appropriate. The only gold material that was suitable at the time was a fabric used in theatrical costuming called lamé. When I suggested it to Skippy, he thought I was brilliant. So, off we went: Skippy and the cocktail waitresses.

At the local costume boutique, we found sexy gold lamé toreador pants and black silk blouses. Gold high heels were to be found in any shoe store back then. We were all set. A nice finishing touch was supplied by Bunny. We passed a notions store and bought gold lamé S's that we sewed onto the black blouses. I couldn't wait for my mother to see me in that outfit.

Skippy and Pat paid for the "uniforms," too. Today, the cost of those outfits would not be expensive, but in 1961, $125 was a lot of money.

Skippy then took us to a French restaurant for lunch. It was my first experience in elegance. The menus had no prices. Everything was plush red velvet, the service impeccable, and the food was like ambrosia. What that lunch cost, I don't know, but I'd be willing to bet it was more than the average man's weekly salary. What a magnificent gesture! God bless you, Skippy, wherever you are.

Pat was so proud of his girls. We were all young and shapely then. Though I was not as pretty as the other three, I had the best figure, and to think I never knew it back then.

I was spared all of the grueling work that went with opening a restaurant. I stayed at the Landmark till the day the Surf opened. I had only once met the girls who were to work with me in the lounge—Bunny, Karen, and Joan Murphy.

To save my soul, I can't remember much about the night the Surf opened. I was to be there at seven o'clock. I remember wanting to get there earlier, as I was very nervous about opening night. There was always heavy traffic on Ocean Avenue (later to be Route 36) in the summer, as all of the beach clubs started to empty around five-thirty. It was a two-lane highway with the ocean on one side and the river on the other side. This strip of land that comprised Sea Bright and Monmouth Beach was at one time referred to as the Normandy Strip. There were very few houses on the side facing the ocean. Houses and boatyards were on the side facing the river. The streets on the river were all dead-end streets since they ended up at the river.

Traveling at a snail's pace on Ocean Avenue, I was startled out of my wits when this huge white car barrel-assed down one of the small side streets. This jerk didn't stop at the stop sign. It was a miracle that he did not hit me, and an even bigger miracle that I did not crash into the seawall on the ocean side.

I was in a state of white heat, brandishing my fist in his face. I called him everything but a child of God. I was so angry; I literally could not see his face. I got out of my car.

Out of the white car stepped this giant of a young man, and he was smiling.

"What the hell are you smiling at, you mutt? If I wasn't in a hurry, I would call the cops."

Not a word from him, just that dazzling smile.

"You must be friggin' drunk." With that, I pushed him with all my strength and sent him crashing against his car. As I drove away, I saw that he was still smiling.

Now, it was a good five miles from the town of Sea Bright, where we had our little altercation, to the Surf in Long Branch, and this nut was following me. Was I afraid? No. I knew that as soon as I got to the Surf, no power in the world could get to me. I prayed he would be stupid enough to follow me there. You got it. He was still behind me when I arrived in the parking lot.

"You gonna get it now, Buster!" I shouted as I ran in the doorway, almost knocking Louie the "Killer" down.

"Frances, what happened?"

God, the comfort of those arms! "Louie, this mutt almost killed me. I hit him, and he followed me here."

Louie rushed down the stairs to "murder the bum." Did he murder him? No. He embraced him! What the hell was going on?

"Frances, there's gotta be a mistake. This is my friend Dickey Kiernan. You know, Sheriff Kiernan's son."

"I don't care of he's *your* son, the son-of-a-bitch is drunk. I'll hit him myself," I bellowed.

Dickey approached me, and he was red in the face. "Please, I'm not drunk, just daydreaming. I stepped on the accelerator instead of the brakes."

I was not convinced and I let him know it. "Why did you follow me then?"

"I wanted to apologize to you, but you knocked the breath out of me when you slammed me against my car."

The whole place cracked up at that. You see, I barely came to his shoulder. I'm five feet five in my stocking feet. Back then, I weighed 115 pounds.

Dickey had a lovely basso-profundo cultured voice. This, coupled with such boyish good looks, undid me. I stuck out my hand to shake his, and we have remained the best of friends to this day.

This little fiasco established me as a "gutsy broad." What nonsense! If it were not for that perfect gentleman, Dickey, I would probably have ended up in the hospital.

At about six-thirty on opening night, the dining room started to fill. This was the group that left the track before the last race. By seven-thirty, it was complete bedlam, wall-to-wall people in the bar, as well as in the dining room. I'm sure I added to the general confusion because I did not know what I was doing.

Charlie Pine, our head bartender, deserved the Purple Heart for putting up with me. I asked a million questions, got the drinks all wrong, picked up someone else's order, and on and on.

Armand Taddio was also behind the main bar. He kept calming me down all night. I was running around like a nut. Eddie Primavera was the third man behind the bar. He kept joking with me, even when I spilled the drinks all over his station. I felt like running out of there.

The girls in the dining room had it worse. They could not get the food out fast enough and, to top it off, they were running out of everything. Pat asked me to help them by serving drinks to their customers.

The first drink order I got was for a Moscow Mule. I had never served one, but I knew it was made with vodka and ginger beer, and it was served warm. Charlie never blinked an eye. "Let's see, it's a Russian drink, so it must have vodka." He fills a large glass with ice, vodka, 7-Up, and I don't know what else.

I told him I couldn't serve it, because it was the wrong drink. He just smiled and said the guy would never know the difference. I was rooted to the spot.

"Look, Frances, if this guy complains, I'll give you fifty dollars. People order drinks that they hear about. They think it's sophisticated. Believe me this guy doesn't know a Moscow Mule from a champagne cocktail."

Of course, he was right. When the customer drank it without a word, I caught Charlie's eye, and we laughed like hell.

At the service bar in the dining room was Louie Garcia, a horse degenerate if there ever was one. All night he kept warning me about taking horse tips from people. He assured me that this was a "bad move." All I would get out of it were empty pockets. I kept telling him that I had never been to a racetrack, that I was not a gambler, and that I had no intention of ever betting on a horse.

Louie Garcia was one of the most pleasant people I have ever had the good fortune to know. He thought I was a strange one, never gambling and all that goes with it, but he liked me in spite of it. I never did learn "horse language," but I made a friend for life.

The rest of the night was a blur, but I do recall that I had a good time. At closing, Skippy and his wife Gloria took all the waitresses to the Monmouth Queen Diner for breakfast. This he continued to do till the day he died. Gloria was a stunning, diminutive, golden blonde. She had blue eyes as large as saucers and a perfectly proportioned figure. She seemed like a remote goddess, but she was warm and friendly. This charming lady remained that way all her life. They made a beautiful couple. To me, they were like movie stars. Life was not kind to Gloria, but she was not bitter or vengeful. She was undaunted. I will not see her like again in this world.

Skippy died at age forty-two, a tragic loss to us all, but a man like that never really dies. He stays alive in the hearts of those who love and cherish his memory.

I remember very little of the first summer at the Surf. Perhaps it was because we were so busy. Every night was like Saturday night. I remember feeling incompetent. The other waitresses had more experience than I had, and they had known one another for years. They were all very nice to me, and very helpful, and surprisingly they did not resent me. After all, I was the newcomer, and I was the head waitress. It seems to me that they should have felt resentment, but they didn't.

That's just the way it was at the Surf. There was no back-stabbing, no petty jealousy, none of the unpleasantness one encounters in the working world. I believe it was due in large measure to Pat Simonetti. He was so fair and impartial; he never reprimanded anyone.

Chapter 5

Pat Simonetti

Pat and his Surf Lounge spoiled me for any other job I ever held. I couldn't wait to get to work. He treated us all as if we were members of his family. More importantly, he trusted us. In all the years I was with him, I never saw him in a bad mood. He was never ruffled if things went wrong. He took everything in good grace. He was always there to help with any problems, even with personal ones.

We worked hard, but we laughed the nights away. Pat was quick to praise you, and he never treated you like a menial. He was the heartbeat of the Surf.

As I said, I was the head waitress in the lounge. I saw the bartenders buying back drinks for their regulars and the spenders. That was Pat's policy, but I was not sure if that applied to me at the tables in the bar.

One night, a stranger came in and kept buying round after round for the people around him. I asked Pat if I could buy his table a round "from the house." The people he sent drinks to had sent back drinks to his table, as well, and I felt sure that since he was spending so much money it was now our turn.

"What are you asking me for?" Pat said. "You are in charge here. You know who to buy for. You feel they should have a drink on the house, buy it."

Like FDR, he knew how to delegate authority. Because he trusted you completely, you could not bring yourself to betray that trust. Also, he was the most tolerant man. He accepted you exactly as you were, with all your warts and beauty marks. I'm ashamed to say that we took advantage of his good nature.

Pat had no enemies; in fact, he was his own worst enemy. He was a compulsive gambler. If he was not, he would have been a millionaire ten times over today. Every restaurant he ever owned was a success. People in the know can tell you it is a hard business; more restaurants fail than succeed.

Pat had panache, a grandeur I have never seen since. Whatever else was wrong with him (he was human after all); pettiness was not one of his faults. He enriched my life. I was a better person for having known him.

During that time, my husband was overseas and would be gone for eighteen months. I decided to put my son, Joe, into a military school. It was only a forty-five-minute drive from my mother's home, but I felt that in a houseful of women, the boy would get more benefit at a boys' school. It was expensive for the times, but I could well afford it.

Now, my husband's allotment check was being held up by some bureaucratic red tape. I told Pat Simonetti that it was just my luck, that for the first time in my marriage I was to get a full allotment check because my husband was in a place where he could not spend money, and the goddamned government was fouling up the works.

Every night, Pat would ask, "Did the check come yet?"

Frank Condi, one of our regular customers, asked what it was all about, and I told him. He thought I was short of money, because I told him my son's uniforms were $450.00. He told me that I should keep my son in the school. He added that his son was spoiled so rotten that he never heard from him unless he needed money. He insisted that I take the money from him for the uniforms. I refused, telling him that I did not need the money.

Everyone thought I was foolish for not taking from Frank, but how could I abuse a friendship like that? Finally, one night he just left the money under his coffee cup. When I tried to give it back, he told me in no uncertain terms that if I insisted, he would never talk to me again. I bought him a gold watch with the money.

The same year was one of Pat's worst gambling seasons. He lost heavily, and our liquor was sent to us C.O.D. He was telling Vinnie the bartender that he was short $300, and there was no one left to borrow from. In I walked and told Vinnie, "Well, the damned allotment check finally came."

The two gazed at each other significantly, and as I was walking away, Vinnie called me, his eyes filled with mischief. "Oh, Frances, Pat wants to talk to you."

The long and the short of it is I paid the liquor bill. Did I feel as if I were being used? Hell no! He would have done the same for me.

My brother-in-law, John, showed up one night with a party of ten. They first went to the bar for a drink, waiting for a table to empty in my station. I introduced Pat to my family. All the regulars were sending drinks to their table, but not Pat.

Now, John was a healthy eater, and he ordered quite a few dishes. Lucille kept sending out her specialties. I told her they didn't order them. "Frances, this is your family. I'm not charging them." It came time for the check, and Pat grabbed it from me. I figured he was going to see if all the items were included.

Vinnie, of course, had to add fat to the fire. "There is a sixteen-dollar bar check there, too."

Pat took the food check and told me, "This they pay." He returned the bar check to me. "I don't pay for anybody's vices." He ripped the food check in half. It was well over a hundred dollars (in those days, a sizeable amount). John, of course, was grateful. He couldn't believe his ears.

He saw Pat drinking like a fish. It was just one of Pat's quirks; he never bought anyone a drink, but customers bought him drinks. He was constantly telling us, "I'll have a drink with Phil Levine" or whoever happened to catch his eye. The only person I ever saw him buy a drink for was my cousin Joey.

That night, when he bought Joey and his party a drink, Maggio was at the bar. He walked over to Joey and said, "Pardon me, are you a faggot?" Joey told him, "No, what makes you think so?"

"Well, I never saw him buy a drink, not even for the most beautiful young girl, so I figure he may be gay, and that you are, too."

I kid you not.

One night, "Black Mike" Avalone came in to borrow two thousand dollars from Pat. Now, Pat had lost at the track that day and he was tapsville. He told Vinnie that his son was in trouble and he had till that night to raise two thousand dollars for bail.

Vinnie looked around the bar, and all the big tippers were there. He smiled at Mike and the light came on. "Give me a pencil and paper," Mike asked. He started to write down everyone's name and the amount he would ask them for, alphabetically mind you. He came to the F's. There was Larry Friedman, a multimillionaire and friend of Mike's. He had Larry down for two hundred dollars.

"You forgot Frances," Vinnie slyly told him. He inserted my name over Larry's and had me down for three hundred dollars. We all give him the amount he had written down for us. Pat magnanimously offered to drive him to Freehold in the morning. He had raised the bail money.

The next night, Big Frank (Mike's boss) came in for dinner. Pat told him of Mike's ingenuity, and Frank asked to see the list. Pat pointed out to him that Larry Friedman was asked for two hundred dollars, and I was asked for three. Frank stopped smiling. He reached into his pocket and handed me three hundred dollars. Turning to Mike, he whispers, "You owe me three hundred."

He knew I would never see my three hundred dollars, and he was pissed. You can be sure that Mike would pay him. Pat was afraid that Mike would get a beating, so he wagged his finger at both of us and said, "You can't tell me you two are not doing something together." Telling him "I'm a washout routine," Frank's good humor was restored. Pat saved the night.

My father, a master of electronics, was working for a firm that did not appreciate him. So, at age fifty, he gave them two weeks' notice and went about looking for another job. I told Pat that my mother, a worry wart, was climbing the walls. She was worried that she was going to the poor house. Pat had no way of knowing there was no danger of that, as my father was not without savings, and a man in his field had no trouble getting work, no matter at what age.

Pat gave me one hundred dollars for my mother to "give her peace of mind" for the moment. Then he told me that my mother and father could eat every night at the Surf to lessen expenses. I told him that they really didn't need anything, but he did not believe me. He thought I was too proud to ask for help.

Every night, he would ask me, "Did your father find a job yet?"

This went on for four weeks. He sent home food to them (which annoyed my father), but I could not convince Pat that they were okay. He asked Pussy if he could find a job for the old man.

Vinnie and I laughed about the whole thing. Vinnie, adding fat to the fire, telling all and sundry, "Poor Frances; her father is out of work."

My mother went to the bank to make her monthly mortgage payment and was told that the mortgage had been paid for must be an error. He did not pay his mortgage six months in advance. The bank showed him the paid receipts. Who paid them? Why, Roberts, Phillsbury, and Carton, the most prestigious law firm in the state of New Jersey, that's who. I knew it was not Pat who paid it, as he was losing heavy at the track.

I found out four years later that Frank had paid it. He did not want any stigma on my father's name, so he paid it through the law firm. Pat had asked him to lend him the money to pay the mortgage, but Frank paid it instead. My father, by the way, did not talk to me for six months.

That was Pat. He had his own money troubles and could not help with what he thought was mine, but he reached out for me. He did things like that for many people.

When the time came that he had to sell the Surf, he was broken-hearted, but he never showed it. He joked about it, telling me "Well, how do you like that? I'm transferring out of my own chicken shit outfit."

He sold the Surf in 1968 and more or less passed out of my life. I remained with the new owners and they were wonderful, but something was missing. Pat, thank God, is still around. He is a man who will remain undaunted. God love him.

Chapter 6

Ray Crow

Ray Crow was a peculiar little guy and a rapid talker. I had to strain to understand what he was saying. In a space of three minutes, he told me that he was a "relief bartender," but he had much more important duties. He was responsible for security. I can honestly say he did not look very formidable to me. I could eat spaghetti off his head.

Ray went on to say that Pat paid him fifty dollars a week, plus free room and board. In addition to this, he was given twenty-five dollars from the bartenders for cleaning up on Sunday morning and getting behind the bar on Sunday till the regulars came to work. What he did not tell me was that the bartenders also gave him a share of their tips, and that he collected fifty-five dollars a week in unemployment.

The biggest perk was that Ray was able to drink all he wanted, free, *gratis*. Poor Ray was an alcoholic. Small enough he was; he surely could put away the booze.

Although Ray was no midget, he bore a strong resemblance to a midget called Johnny, who advertised for the Phillip Morris

Company in the early 1950s. That Johnny was dressed like a bellhop, and he would walk through a hotel lobby with a small tray carrying a pack of Phillip Morris cigarettes, saying, "Call for Phillip M-o-r-r-i-s."

Ray's hair was black as a crow, and he had cornflower blue eyes. He had small features and beautiful teeth. He was quite nice looking. I liked this little man on sight. He confided in me that he was "in between jobs," and that before the drink got him, he had been a "big book in Cuba." For the unenlightened, a "book" is a bookmaker.

"It wasn't only the drink that did me in," he confessed. "Castro, that mutt, took over and I had to go on the lam (go into hiding). They are still looking for me."

I wondered why Castro with all his troubles was looking for Ray.

"No, no, not Castro! The FBI is looking for me!"

I later learned that Ray had indeed been a bookmaker in Cuba. As for the FBI, they would not have known him if they fell over him.

One of his self-appointed jobs was answering the phone in the lobby. It never failed to amuse us when he said, "Hello, Soif." Now, Ray had good diction, so saying Soif instead of Surf was his idea of how a gangster would speak. In ten years, I could not get him to pronounce it correctly.

Another self-appointed job was "screening the customers." If he spotted a non-regular, he would approach that person and then, snarling in their face, demand "Who are you? State your business." Surprisingly, no one took offense at this. You see, Ray had delusions of grandeur. He imagined that he was an Al Capone-type living in the Roaring Twenties. The *real* Al Capone types got a big kick out of Ray and went along with it. They had great compassion for him and always built up his ego by telling him what a great job he was doing protecting the "joint."

When a figure high up in the crime world told him "You're my main man," he was on Cloud 9. No one ever ridiculed him. They liked the little guy and went to considerable lengths to shield him from unkind people. They instinctively knew that to damage his pride would kill him; this, from men who were considered the "dregs of society."

I don't know if Ray had any family. If he did, he never mentioned them. The love of his life was a girl named Cathy. Whenever she needed money, she would come around to see him. Each time, she would stay long enough to drain him and then leave again. When this happened, the poor guy would go into depression that was awful to see. That low-life girl kept him destitute. He never realized we knew this, and he went to great subterfuge borrowing money. Mostly he "borrowed" from Vinnie the bartender and me.

Jackie Leonard, the late great comedian, was a frequent customer of ours. He stayed at the Harbor Island Spa down the street from us in a vain attempt to lose weight. Lots of who's who in the entertainment world were guests of the spa. Jackie became a personal friend of the "gang." He told us that Ray Crow was a "greater wit and ad-libber than Groucho Marx." I, for one, would not dispute him. Ray missed his calling. He would have been one of the great comedians of our time. Of course, he did not have the dedication it takes to become a star. He would rather have been Al Capone.

One night Vinnie called me over to tell me that Ray needed forty-two dollars to "take his clothes out of the tailors."

Now, I am not the brightest light in the world, but it didn't take a genius to figure out that in 1962, $42.00 was a bit high for a cleaning bill. "Jesus Christ, Vinnie, this guy must have more clothes than Adolph Menjue."

That outburst established me as a great wit. Of course, Cathy was back in town. Vinnie offered to split the debt. He felt sorry for me, because I was a soft touch. This pattern of splitting the money Ray "borrowed" lasted almost fifteen years. We never minded. After all, how do you thank a man for a million laughs?

As I explained previously, the Surf was an old boarding house. There were several bedrooms on the third floor. Ray, Victor our janitor, and Victor's cat occupied two of them. Ray hated and feared the cat. Victor, poor soul, was mildly retarded, but mostly harmless. The only thing that could rile Victor was unkindness toward his cat. We knew the danger signals. If Victor was mumbling, watch out!

There was much animosity between the two because of the cat. Now, the cat only frightened Ray; Victor, however, terrified him.

In order to sleep nights, Ray got hold of a gun. What good this gun was I'll never know, because Pat would never allow him to have any bullets. Since the gun gave him comfort, he was allowed to keep it. Possessing the gun helped with Ray's illusion that he was a "wise guy," Mob vernacular for gangster.

We ran out of dinner rolls one busy night, and Pussy's brother-in-law Lindy volunteered to get some more. Not wanting to drive alone, he called to Ray, who was sleeping upstairs. "I need you, Buddy."

Down like a shot Ray came. "Here I am, Chief. Let's go." As he walked towards the door, he stopped dead in his tracks. "We can't go yet. I forgot the piece," he said without a trace of a smile.

Lindy whispered, "Ray, we're only going to get some rolls." This, of course, went over Ray's head.

Later that night, while cleaning the bar, we heard a loud gunshot coming from Ray's room. Ray must have bought bullets when he and Lindy were out buying rolls. Mistaking Victor's cat for a large rat, Ray had shot at it and grazed his own foot in the process. Thank God for that. How could we have explained a gunshot wound? Coming from the Surf, the papers would have had a field day.

Poor Victor was convinced that Ray was trying to kill his cat. After that incident, no bullets were ever allowed in Ray's possession, but how to protect him from Victor's hatred?

The best we could do was to put all kinds of locks on Ray's door and join forces in seeing that the two were never alone in each other's company. It wasn't until Ray got himself a room at the Landmark that we relaxed our vigil. Pussy continued to pay Ray's rent secretly from 1963 till Pat sold the place in 1969.

Lots of people in the Surf were addicted to racetrack betting. I was not among them, but Ray was at the top of the list. Not far behind him was Peter Salomida, who owned a very successful used car lot and earned the nickname "Car Lot Pete." He was shy and gentle with a cherubic face.

I used to love teasing him. I was pretty good at imitating Bette Davis, and I used to crack him up when, in my best Bette Davis voice, I would greet him with "Peter, don't be bitter. If it's anything I cannot stand it is a bitter Peter." He had me do this little routine over and over for his family and friends. He rewarded me for this by naming a horse after me. Yes, he owned horses, too. None ever made it to the Derby, but Peter never went broke.

My namesake was running a race, and Peter insisted I go to the track with him that day "for luck." Though I had never been to Monmouth Park, I had many friends there—trainers, jockeys, and racing fans.

We arrived early so we could go to the paddock to see "Francie." We met Budd Lepman on the way there. Budd was one of the top trainers in the country, a very courtly gentleman, but a devil when it came to ordering food. Though never rude, he was at times very cranky. I called him "Mother." That was half a word to describe him when he was at his absolute worst. He, in turn, called me the same. We were the best of friends.

"Mother," he asked, "what are you doing here? You never bet."

I explained about the horse and could not resist teasing him by telling that Peter and I went broke. He put his hand in his pocket and thrust a few hundred dollars at me. "For Christ's sake, it's only 10 a.m. We can't bet for three hours yet. Take back your gold; it could never buy me."

I kissed him goodbye and was immediately surrounded by strangers asking me, "What horse did he give you?"

"I never asked him for a horse," I replied.

"Why not?" they retorted.

"You mean the horses tell him who will win?" I was half-serious.

Peter explained that the trainers often were in a position to predict a winning horse with certain accuracy. I could not have cared less. Budd was my friend. I would never have taken advantage of that friendship. This generous man was forever showering me with money, so why in the world would I have to bet on a horse?

We were watching the playback of the first race, when we ran into Ray Crow. Throwing his arms around me, he shouted, "Holy Christ, Frannie! Thank God I ran into you. I'm tapped. Can you help me with a ten-spot?"

Being no stranger to his needs, I gave him ten dollars. Peter meanwhile was laughing hysterically.

"What the hell is so funny about helping the little guy?" I barked at him.

Wiping the tears from his eyes, he said, "No, nothing. But did your friend come to the track with three dollars?" This witticism was lost on me, so he went on to explain. "Frannie, the second race did not start yet, and he is broke?" I told him about poor Ray, and he was all apologies. The horse Ray bet on, of course, lost, so we left the track to get supper.

We were stopped at a red light in front of Moran's Bar when out dashed Ray. "Holy Christ, Frannie, it's a miracle seeing you. Can you bail me out? I'm tapped."

This time it was Peter who did the honor. He gave him twenty dollars. For the next fifteen years, Ray asked to be bailed out, especially if I was in the company of moneyed men. I refused to believe that he was using me. I knew he was a poor unfortunate that could not hold onto a dollar.

It took Pat Merola, one of our regular customers, to make me understand that I was not helping Ray. Pat told me that no matter how much I gave to Ray, he would always need more. Don't misunderstand me. I was making a lot of money and didn't mind helping others. Pat's argument was that gamblers, alcoholics, and junkies (we did not see very many of these, because Pussy frowned on the dope scene) are weak people; by giving them money you only help them feed their habits.

My argument was that the strong would help the weak. Pat, wise soul that he was, won the argument by pointing out that the strong do not pull the weak up; the weak pull the strong down.

Pat's wife was an alcoholic, and he was a tortured man. He was the only one that knew I was in the same boat. My husband was on his way to becoming an alcoholic, if he wasn't already there.

But this is Ray's chapter, so on with the story.

At the Surf, the crew was fed before the dining room opened. We had our own table, and Pat Merola ate with us quite frequently. One particular night, "Lucky" Lavoie came in to pay back hundreds of dollars he had borrowed from me. Ray noted this and was ready. He called me aside and asked for a loan of a hundred dollars. "All I need is $100 to straighten myself out."

Of course, I gave it to him. Pat took all of this in (he missed very little) and was miffed at me. "You are a stubborn woman. Next week, all he will need will be $200 to straighten himself out. You have two kids to care for. Nothing will help this man."

He was off by $100. The following week, Ray needed only $300. That night Pat took the bull by the horns. Calling Ray and me to the bar at closing time, he handed Ray $500. "Here, this money is a gift. You do not have to pay it back. Get yourself straightened out once and for all."

You guessed it! A month later, he needed only a thousand dollars. I learned my lesson. From that day forward, the largest amount of money I would give him was fifty dollars. If I saw him today, I would still give him money. So would everyone else, for that matter. Ray was not only loved; he was cherished.

I could go on and on with stories about Ray, but there are so many others to tell you about that it would be unfair to leave them out. However, before we leave Ray, there are two more tales I must tell since they are at the top of the heap.

Ray, as I pointed out, had delusions of grandeur. He never forgot his salad days when he was a big book in Cuba. Through the years, he imagined himself to be a wise guy. No one minded this little deception. I had a few of my own.

In the early days, it was the crew's habit to go for breakfast after closing. The crew included Helen, the head waitress in the dining room, and most of the other waitresses. We were at the Sun and Shore one night when a man, fascinated by Helen's startling resemblance to Liz Taylor, snapped her picture. The flashbulb went off, and the excitable Ray shouted, "Holy Christ! The FBI is after me. What a shot I got!"

Why, he was no more wanted by the FBI than Mother Theresa was. The poor man who took the picture kept saying, "Please, sir, calm down. I was not taking your picture. I wanted the young lady's picture."

No use; the man could not convince him that he was only a tourist. Poor Ray started "borrowing" money all over the place, explaining that he had to go on the lam. Sure enough, he went missing for about three weeks. Pussy was so worried about him that he sent all his men out to look for him. They found him in

Asbury Park, three miles south of Long Branch! I guess if you really want to hide, you stay out in the open.

Last, but not least, is the story that keeps me laughing till this day. It happened on the Fourth of July weekend, one of the busiest nights of the summer season. "Big Frank" Condi, Surf regular, told me that he was waiting for "three important men" but that he had to leave for a few minutes. He asked if I would seat them at his table till he returned. For some reason or other, Ray missed this conversation (he didn't miss many), and the comedy of errors occurred.

I was so busy running in and out of the kitchen that I missed the men as they came in. Ray spotted them immediately. He knew all the regulars, and these men were strangers. Approaching them with extreme suspicion (as Ray did with all strangers), and in his best James Cagney gangster voice, he asked if he could help them.

"We're looking for Frank," they politely told him.

"Frank who?" he sneered. "Who are you? State your business here."

The strangers dropped their polite demeanor and replaced it with real menace. The real gangsters were very annoyed.

"OK, Buster. Answer my question or out you go."

At that exact moment, Frank, thank God, came to the door. I was sure that Ray was a goner. Running to Frank, I screamed, "Hurry! Those guys will squash him like an egg!"

He took it all in at a glance. "Good job, Ray. I never worry when you are at the door."

Ray came up to the armpit of the shortest of the three strangers. Apologizing, Frank explained that Ray was only doing his job. Now, they were dumbfounded. Leading them to the table, he briefly explained Ray's story. Now, it was their turn to apologize. They assured Frank that they would make it up to the little guy.

When they left, the toughest-looking one gave Ray fifty dollars. He even went one better. He told Ray, "Pal, I wish I had a guy like you in my organization. My guys are all pussycats. If ever you decide to leave this organization, look me up."

The man must have been a real "big shot" because Ray was on Cloud 9 for months. Frank was the "real McCoy." A captain and nobody to mess with, he was an extremely masculine man, very handsome, and never a bully. In fact, he went out of his way to protect the small and the meek. It was only when he had too much to drink that he was a little nasty, but we were never truly afraid of him.

Chapter 7

Smokey & Cheech

Smokey was the chef at the Surf the first year it was open, and Cheech was his assistant. Smokey was of Italian descent; Cheech was a black man, who had been "christened" with his nickname, which is Italian for Frank. The two worked well together. Smokey was a temperamental culinary genius. Cheech was a quiet, good-natured man and more of a real culinary genius.

Smokey was a real lady's man. He had a pleasant face with a nose that Jimmy Durante would have envied. Because I was in the cocktail lounge in the early days, I was seldom in the kitchen. We could serve sandwiches at the bar, but only after the dinner hour. This protected me from Smokey's wrath; nevertheless, I was afraid of him. Under pressure, he could be extremely ugly. He was not too friendly with me, my being the "new kid on the block." All of the other waitresses had worked with him before, so they were not intimidated by him.

Cheech, on the other hand, bent over backwards to be nice to everyone. He adored Pat, and Pat loved him in return. I was never afraid of Cheech.

Pat spoiled his customers shamefully. "Give them anything they want" was his motto. They took advantage of this by constantly ordering items that were not on the menu. Smokey would go berserk when these orders came to him. I had no way of knowing if this was a trial for the cooks, but Pat was the boss, so I did what he told me to do.

The word got around, "If you want something different, ask Frances." This endeared me to the customers, but it went over like a lead fart in the kitchen. It did not sit too well with the other waitresses, either. Considering all this, I have to say that Smokey was not really vicious towards me. When he realized that I was not being a "smart ass," just a dumb bunny, we became fast friends. It was Pussy who, unawares, made it happen.

I was suffering from anemia back then. This left me tired and listless, but I managed somehow to keep going. Pussy was concerned, having a blood problem himself. He was very compassionate. He advised me to eat liver and red meats. Preferring pasta, I did not take his advice. In this battle of wills, it was Pussy who won.

I went into the kitchen and ordered a steak, very rare, for my dinner that night. Smokey flew into a rage. "Who the fuck do you think you are? You will eat what I cook for the help. If you offered to pay double for it, I would not cook you a steak. Get the fuck out of my kitchen!"

Pussy heard him. Indeed, half of Long Branch must have heard him. Walking into the kitchen, Pussy placed his finger on Smokey's nose. In a deadly calm voice, he whispered, "You give her anything she wants, and remember this; you'll go before she goes." It was like a scene in a western movie when the bad man walks into the saloon. Dead silence.

Without uttering a word, the steak was prepared for me. The damned thing went down my throat like sawdust. I felt so bad for Smokey. I wanted the earth to open up and swallow me.

At work the next day, Smokey asked me why I didn't tell him that I was Pussy's girl. For a second, it didn't register. I wasn't Pussy's girl, for God's sake. Mrs. (Rose) Russo had more affection for me than he had. Oh, he liked me, but he liked us all. Rose loved only me. She made this clear the next night when she and Pussy came in for a late night snack. His check came to some forty-nine dollars. He paid it with a hundred-dollar bill and told me to keep the change.

Hearing this, Rose became visibly angered. "How much money did you give her?" she hissed at him. (Dear God, did she also think I was Pussy's girl?)

Pussy, in turn, was stunned; she never questioned anything he did. "I gave her fifty dollars," he meekly replied.

"You give fifty dollars to everybody. To her, you should give more."

I protested, telling her that a fifty-dollar tip was too generous.

"No, Rose is right," he said. "To you, I should give more. He handed me another fifty dollars.

This incident told one and all that I was more than a girlfriend. I was a valued, respected person. Please do not misunderstand.

Some of the girlfriends were in meaningful relationships, but most were not. I believe most of the girlfriends were status symbols. *Look at me! I can afford this beautiful young girl.*

Pussy, that rogue, had them all over the United States. We were constantly receiving collect calls for Mr. Russo from his "niece" in Boston, New York, Chicago…you name it. The man never ate a meal in peace. One particular night, the calls were heavier than ever. I yanked the phone out of the wall and said, "Now, eat! Who do you think you are, King Farouk?"

His underlings were startled by my boldness; they waited for the axe to fall. Flashing his radiant smile, Pussy calmly answered, "Farouk you, too."

But I am digressing from Smokey and Cheech. More about Pussy and his amours later.

The dining room waitresses had to be at work at 4 p.m. in order to prepare for the dinner crowd. The girls in the lounge did not have to be there until 8:30 p.m. I always arrived by 7 p.m., because I enjoyed helping the girls at the peak of the dinner hour. I would clear tables, get their cocktail orders, and just make myself useful. In the beginning, this was resented. They thought I was hustling their tables. In time, they came to know this was not the case at all. All through the years at the Surf, we were inseparable. Pussy dubbed us the "Filthy Four."

The kitchen fascinated me. I love to cook, and here was an opportunity to learn new recipes. I would go into the kitchen and clean lettuce, peel potatoes, run errands, and so forth. In time, in spite of the thousand questions I asked, Smokey warmed up to me. I was a collector of cookbooks; then I had about fifty. Today they number over eight hundred, most of them gifts from the Mob.

Cheech was the most imitative cook I ever knew. He had to taste a dish only once, and he could duplicate it. Few could tell if Cheech or Smokey was cooking that night. Taking advantage of this fact, Smokey would slip out at night to meet some girl.

Pat Simonetti very seldom came into the kitchen after 9 o'clock. He was too busy singing with the band or just chatting with the customers. Of course, Smokey's sneaking out could not go on indefinitely. Pat was bound to find out sooner or later.

Smokey's big mistake was leaving before 9 p.m. Pat walked into the kitchen, and no Smokey. Cheech played dumb, and Pat was exasperated with him, as if it was his fault.

Fiery-tempered Helen came to his rescue. "What are you hollering at him for?" she lashed out at Pat. "Stop abusing him! This has been going on for the last six months. If you paid attention to what's going on instead of singing on the stage, you would know what's going on!"

Pat was stunned. He apologized. When Smokey left to open his own restaurant shortly after that (Pat never fired anyone), Cheech became the chef.

The amazing Cheech was a tireless worker. He was lame, a condition that resulted from a tragedy that could have been prevented. When he was a little boy of nine in North Carolina, he broke his leg. The family was too poor to pay a doctor, so the leg never set right. In the process of growing up, the leg remained crooked. In spite of being very lame and in a great deal of pain, he never sat down during working hours. Cheech never complained. He was always so agreeable. In addition, he was never out sick. He was so punctual that if he was ten minutes late, we became very worried.

He had three children and a wife who could have given lessons to Lucretia Borgia. At the time, they were separated but we knew nothing of this. Cheech was a very private person. It was many years later that we learned of all he had suffered with this bitch. It all came to light when Cheech just disappeared for three weeks.

Pussy was very alarmed; he feared that Cheech might have met with foul play, since he was not a drinker or gambler. Cheech had relatives in Newark, and Pussy's men were sent there to find him.

When Pussy told me this, I laughed in his face.

"What's so funny, you *Sigi* bastard? I'm worried about the guy."

Being of Sicilian descent, I was a *Sigi* to him. My God, the man was naïve! "Oh, boss, think about it. You send a bunch of torpedoes into the black section of Newark looking for him? Of course, they will close ranks to protect him."

This went over his head, so I continued. "Look at it this way. You are a black man in hiding. The word is out that Pussy Russo is looking for you. Of course, they think you mean to harm him, so they are not going to tell your men where he is."

Grabbing me in a bear hug and kissing me on the head, he jubilantly cried out, "I wouldn't take a sack of gold for you and that fucking brain of yours."

Taking matters into his own hands, he personally approached a black leader in Newark. Explaining that he loved Cheech and feared that he was in some kind of trouble, he wanted to help him.

In a short time, Cheech appeared. It seems that he had fallen behind in his child support payments, because of his mother's medical bills. His miserable wife had signed a complaint against him, knowing full well that he would go without in order to pay her in full as soon as he could. He sent bags of groceries to her every day, and welfare was paying the rent, but she wanted him in jail. Naturally, he ran away.

Knowing that Cheech had a lot of pride and would never have approached Pussy for the money, he handled the whole thing beautifully.

"You mean to tell me that for a lousy fifteen hundred dollars, you made me eat garbage for two months?" Pussy asked. "Cheech, I thought you liked me better than that. Please, if, God forbid, it should happen again, come to me right away. I'm liable to be poisoned or worse."

He not only gave him the money, he settled her hash for all time. Sending for the wife, he told her that if ever the money for the kids fell behind, she should contact him right away and he would pay it. He warned her about going to the police. He then did something that went against his grain. He threatened her, telling her that if she ever did anything to harm Cheech or the kids, she would "find herself in an ashtray."

You see, these "criminals" never bullied anyone in an indefensible position. They did not "make war" on women or children. In a sense they were fifteenth century men. Womanhood and motherhood were sacred. In all the history of organized crime, no mother was ever harmed in retaliation for her son's wrongdoing. Even during gang wars in the 1920s and 1930s, when the families of the warring gangs were "hit" in retaliation, the mothers could cross barriers in complete safety. Only two infractions of these "rules and codes" justified a murder—a "made" man fooling around with the wife of another "made" man and informing on a member of organized crime. There is no denying that many murders were committed but they were not "sanctioned."

Cheech, I am sorry to say, treated me rather shabbily in the 1980s. He was not justified in doing so, but I understood his reasons and I still do not hold it against him. I am sorry it happened; he lost a valuable friend. I will not go into it, because it is our secret.

As for Smokey, he opened an Italian restaurant called the Pompey. It did not interfere with the Surf's business. His restaurant did not serve liquor, and food was served till 5 a.m.

The Surf's crew always went to breakfast after closing. Most nights, after the Surf closed and the crew went out to breakfast, Pat Merola treated one and all, usually at the Pompey. Those were the days. We had so much fun with Pat. He was the prankster to beat all pranksters. He would "accidentally" spill water on some innocent person and then goad them into insulting him. The outraged victim would, of course, spill water on him, and the water fight was on. Pretty soon, all the customers would be throwing water at one another. It was all done in fun. No one got mad about it, not even poor Smokey.

The best sport of all was Andy Gerard. The impeccable Andy was not only drenched with water, he was also sprinkled with bits of tomato on his five-hundred-dollar suit. His sister in turn had a beautiful fur stole ruined. Pat, of course, bought her another one. Was Andy angry? No. He went into the kitchen, got a can of whipped cream, and sprayed Pat with it. Pat ducked, and "Big Alfrey" got it all. Everyone had a good time.

Pat always left plenty of money with Smokey to pay for the damages. I guess we got out of hand one night because we were told to be at the Surf two hours earlier. Pussy was holding a meeting. Word had reached him of our clowning around. It was harming Smokey's business. Since Pussy was the gambling boss of Monmouth County, it was up to him to straighten things out.

Arriving at the Surf, we found Pussy pacing back and forth like a caged lion. He was in as black a mood as I had ever seen him. "Sit down, you bunch of clowns," he bellowed. "What are you, a bunch of middle-aged adolescents?"

I could understand the others and me being cowed, but Pat, too? He was a boss in his own right. He was to Essex County what Pussy was to Monmouth County. Why was he taking all this verbal abuse?

Later it was explained to me that Pat was not afraid of Pussy. He remained silent because he knew Pussy was right. Also, Pussy was older. In the circle they belonged to, one respected an older person, whether they were right or wrong.

Pussy went on to say that we were worse than people who robbed widows and orphans, "taking the bread out of a working man's mouth."

This was too much for me to swallow, so I gave him a Bronx "raspberry."

He waited for the snickering to die down, and then he pounced on me. "You got anything to say, big mouth?"

You may wonder why I got away with such disrespect. Pussy admired "gutsy people," and I was pretty gutsy in those days. Of course, I had the advantage. I was a woman, and a woman his wife loved. In the eyes of our world, I was made of glass.

"Yes, I have plenty to say. If Smokey is so pissed off, why didn't he tell Pat? He had no qualms about taking the money that Pat showered on him."

Would I never learn to shut my big mouth?

"It's always you, smart ass. Well, for your information, Smokey did not rat on you. His other customers complained to me about it and how it was harming his business, so if you can't behave like civilized people, stay the hell out of there."

He was no longer shouting. He was whispering. Even I knew better than to answer him when he was whispering. We all felt ashamed of ourselves and gave our solemn promise that we would behave better in the future.

The road to hell is paved with good intentions, it is said, and that is a fact. We continued our shenanigans, of course. From the day the Surf opened to the day it closed, Pat Merola was welcomed in every restaurant in Monmouth County, but nothing could induce the restaurateur to serve him whipped cream in any way, shape, or form.

As for Smokey, we remain good friends to the present day. If he opened a restaurant in Afghanistan, I would do my darndest to go there.

Chapter 8

Chef Lucille

By the second year, Lucille had become chef at the Surf. While nowhere near Smokey in temperament, she had her moments. Over the years, we all took advantage of Pat's good nature, but Lucille was the worst offender.

Sal Russo was one of our favorite entertainers. He and his group were a constant attraction at the Surf. At that time, he was playing in a bar in Asbury Park, and Lucille wanted to see him. That night, she rushed her work in the kitchen to get through early.

As fate would have it, we got a last-minute call for a dinner reservation. Lucille was furious. "I'm not staying! Let Frankie take care of them."

Pat Simonetti pleaded with her because the customers had requested her. We knew he would move heaven and earth for his customers. Lucille stormed out of the kitchen and barked at me, "Come on, we're leaving." I had promised to go with her, so I could not back out.

Turning to us, he shouted at Lucille, "You can't go."

"Who said so?"

"I did."

"Who are you?"

"I'm the boss."

"Fuck you!"

"You can't talk to me like that. I'm the boss."

"Oh, you're the boss. Well, fuck you again."

With that, she turned her back to Pat and propelled me out the door.

"If you two leave now, you're fired," Pat yelled.

Off we went. We saw the Sal Russo show and went back to the Surf. As we were seated at the bar, Pat came over and fired us again.

"Fuck him, Frances. Let's go to the Banjo Palace."

Off we went again. Nothing was doing at the Banjo, so we returned to the Surf. Vinnie told all the guys at the bar that Pat fired us five times that night. Lucille was restless and wanted to go bouncing again. Pat was still pissed at us and as we got up to leave, he fired us again.

Vitamins, that devil, got everyone at the bar to pretend they were following us out the door.

"Where are you guys going?" Pat was desperate.

"You fired Frances and Lucille, so we're leaving, too," Vitamins informed him.

"Wait, wait! They are hired again."

Poor Pat, if I were him, I would have killed both of us.

Tuesday night was Frank Condi's "night out with the boys," so we girls would play cards with his wife Trudy at their home. It was poker, cut-throat at that, and too rich for my blood, and so most of the time, I just made coffee and watched TV while they played.

Lucille was a big gambler and a very sore loser but win or lose she never really lost at Frank's house. He would return home by the time the game broke up. One look at Lucille's face, and he would know she lost that night. He would get her in a corner and ask how much she lost, and whatever the amount, he would "make it good" and reimburse her. She played it for all it was worth. She stopped at nothing, not even his furniture.

In Lu's apartment, everything was Early American. Frank had a lovely grandfather clock, and Lu wanted it badly. One night, he just gave her the damned clock and, what's more, he paid to have it delivered to her.

When I told him he was a "mark," he denied it. He told me that he was afraid that if Lu really got mad at his house, she might spit in his food. Well, Lu was a terror, but she would never have done that. No convincing Frank; he just kept shelling it out.

One night, to celebrate nothing in particular, Pat Simonetti decided to take us all to Mrs. J's, one of his favorite haunts in Asbury Park. No one made key lime pie like Mrs. J.

She was one of the first people to have go-go girls dancing in cages on her stage. By the time we got there, the entertainment was finished. The cages were empty.

"Go up and dance in the cage," Lucille ordered me.

I was not interested. Pat Merola, that instigator, told Lucille that I said she was too fat to dance.

"Oh, yeah?" Lu said. "If she gets up to dance, so will I."

What the hell. I went to one of the cages, and Lucille to the other. We were doing our best to imitate the go-go girls. Everybody was having a great time. As we were getting out of the cages, Lucille came crashing down the steps. It sounded like an earthquake.

Mrs. J. was frantic. "Are you all right, Lucille?" she crooned. "Come have some of my key lime pie."

Seeing that she was almost in tears, Pat walked up to her and with a straight face he said, "Never mind, Mrs. J. My attorneys will be here in the morning. When my chef went up there, she was a virgin."

It took a minute to sink in but she was now relaxed.

I asked Lu how she fell. "My sandal broke. Help me find my other one." To this day, the other sandal has never turned up. Thank God, she landed on her rear end; there were no bones there. All night long, she kept saying, "I hurt the cheeks of my arse."

Cheeks or no cheeks, the next night she was at her post in the kitchen.

Nanay was a boss, the head of Murder, Inc. He and I would meet at Mike's on the boardwalk. Lucille would always get there ahead of us. She would eat several hot dogs and order food to go for Gigi, her mother's standard poodle. Naturally, being Lu, she would put the food on Nanay's tab. He never minded. He was soft spoken, kindly, and humorous. Go, figure.

The Surf Recipes

Chef Lucille's Original & Adapted Recipes

An hour before opening, the staff at the Surf ate whatever Lucille prepared for us. It was like reform school. On Monday, we ate her Meatball Stew, which was a delicious soup, not a stew. Tuesday and Thursday were pasta days. On Wednesday, we had chili. Friday we always ate fish, and on Saturday, we had steak, pork chops or lamb chops, always some kind of meat. She served her meals with her daily choice of vegetables and a salad.

This menu did not vary for eighteen years. I have broken down the following recipes to serve four (4).

Pussy's Orange Appetizer

1 large eating orange, sliced ⅛ of an inch thin
Olive oil
Salt
Red pepper flakes

Spread a thin coating of olive oil over orange slices.
Lightly sprinkle salt and red pepper flakes over the tops.
Refrigerate for an hour before serving.

[NOTE: This was a Sicilian delicacy. Pussy, of course, denied it, as he supposedly hated all things Sicilian. Most of our guys asked him how he could eat "that shit." He said that it made him extra potent sexually. Pat quipped, "After that, I found it hard to locate an orange in Monmouth County."]

Lucille's Meatballs

1 pound, each, ground beef, pork, and veal
¼ cup grated Parmigiano cheese
2 cloves garlic, finely chopped
1 Tablespoon fresh parsley, minced
1 cup Italian bread crumbs
Salt and pepper, to taste
4 eggs, beaten until frothy
½ cup milk
Using your hands, mix all ingredients until well blended.
Shape into meatballs the size of large walnuts.

Use in Meatball Stew recipe that follows.

Meatball Stew

Olive oil, about 1 cup
4 potatoes
4 carrots
1 cup peas
1 cup string beans
1 cup white beans

Cut potatoes and carrots into uniform pieces.
Lightly brown them in olive oil.
Add peas and both kinds of beans.
Add two cups water, and bring to a boil.
Simmer.
When vegetables are still crunchy, add meatballs to the pot.
Simmer 1 hour.
If fresh basil is available, add a generous handful to the pot.

Chili

1 pound, chuck, cut into medium cubes
1 Tablespoon chili powder
1 Tablespoon cumin
1 Tablespoon cilantro
1 large can Italian plum tomatoes, chopped finely
1 large Spanish onion
3 cloves garlic, minced
1 teaspoon oregano
Handful fresh basil leaves
1 large can cannelloni beans
1 small can refried beans
Salt and black pepper, to taste

Chop the onion coarsely.
In large frying pan, brown the meat, onions, and garlic.
Set aside.
In medium pot, place tomatoes.
Add chili powder, cumin, and cilantro.
Bring to a boil.
Add refried beans and stir.
Simmer slowly for one hour.
Add meat, onions, and garlic.
Simmer one-half hour.
Add cannelloni beans.
Add chili powder, salt, and pepper.
Simmer ½ hour.
When beans and meat are tender, cover pot.
Let stand for half an hour.

Meat Sauce for Pasta

[NOTE: Lucille always used plum tomatoes canned in San Marinzano, Italy. The Sclafani brand was the best. The company was located in Boston, and in the 1960s when the Surf was going strong, Mr. Sclafani himself delivered our orders. This was because Lucille fed him. How he enjoyed her cooking! He once told her that the finest olive oil in the world came from Spain; Goya is the only one I see today, and it is very good. But I digress.]

2 cans Italian plum tomatoes
1 cup chicken stock
2 cans tomato paste (Hunt's is the best, believe it or not)
3 cloves garlic
1 Tablespoon salted capers (soak in cold water for a few hours, discard water)
1 Tablespoon fresh oregano
Handful of basil leaves
10 meat balls
½ pound Italian sausage
2 pork neck bones

Drain plum tomatoes. Save liquid. [Lucille always added this to the water that she used to boil the pasta.]
In large bowl, crush tomatoes.
Add 1 cup chicken stock.
In medium pot, sauté garlic, capers, basil, and oregano in olive oil until garlic is yellow. Do not brown!
Add crushed tomatoes and bring to soft boil.
Simmer one hour.
Add tomato paste.
Brown the meatballs, sausage, and neck bones.
Add neck bones to pot and bring to slow boil.
Cook neck bones one-half hour.
Add meatballs and Italian sausage and bring to soft boil.
Lower heat and simmer 1 hour.
If sauce is too thick, add 1 cup chicken stock.
Simmer another one-half hour. Cover pot and turn off heat.

Marinara Sauce

This sauce is the same as the recipe above, but without the meat and tomato paste. Use the same ingredients, otherwise.

[NOTE: There are many different shapes of pasta and almost as many varieties of sauces. The marriage of the right pasta with the right sauce was an art that Lucille mastered. It really improved the taste of the finished dishes.]

Spaghetti with Sun-Dried Tomatoes and Goat Cheese

[NOTE: When Sicilian goat cheese was not available, Lucille used Montrachet.]

¼ cup olive oil
½ cup tomatoes, peeled and chopped into small pieces
½ ounce goat cheese
¼ pound oil-cured, sun-dried tomatoes, coarsely chopped with the oil
1 Tablespoon Italian parsley, finely chopped
30 large basil leaves
2 oz. prosciutto, fat trimmed, thinly sliced into dime-sized pieces
Black pepper, to taste
1 lb. spaghetti

Have all ingredients ready.
Cook spaghetti until tender.
Drain spaghetti, saving ½ cup of pasta water.
Put spaghetti in pot on stove over warm heat.
Add ingredients in the following order: olive oil, fresh tomatoes, goat cheese.
If pasta is dry or sticks together in lumps, add reserved pasta water, a little at a time until mixture becomes smoother.
Add sun-dried tomatoes, parsley, basil, prosciutto, and pepper.
Toss until all ingredients are thoroughly mixed.
Enjoy!

Bucatini with Tomatoes & Purple Onions

¼ cup olive oil
¼ lb. pancetta, thickly sliced, then diced into ½-inch pieces

[NOTE: Pancetta is Italian bacon; if not available, regular bacon can be used.]

1 teaspoon crushed red pepper
2 large cans tomatoes, drained (reserve juice)
½ lb. purple onion, chopped
1 lb. Bucatini (thick, hollow spaghetti-type pasta) or Perciatelli (thick tubular pasta)
Grated Perorino or Locatelli cheese, for use at the table

In 1 Tablespoon olive oil, cook pancetta over medium-high heat for about 5 to 10 minutes, stirring constantly until the pieces are crisp.
Pour off any excess fat.
Add remaining ingredients: olive oil, pepper, and onion.
Continue sautéing until the onion is soft, about another 5 minutes.
Add tomatoes and sauté one more minute.
Lower heat, cover pot, and simmer 20 minutes, stirring occasionally to keep sauce from sticking.
Cook pasta until about three-fourths done.
Drain and toss with liquid from the tomatoes.
Let set on low heat, stirring now and then until all excess liquid from the tomatoes has been absorbed and pasta is tender.
Serve with grated cheese.

Penne San Vito à la Lucille

1 teaspoon crushed red pepper
1 clove garlic, minced or pressed
½ cup olive oil
2 cups chopped onions
¼ lb. tomatoes, peeled and chopped
¼ lb. oil-cured, sun-dried tomatoes, cut into Penne-size slices
½ lb. arugula, chopped
9 large oil-cured green olives, pitted and coarsely chopped
1 lb. penne pasta
½ lb. ricotta salata cheese, thinly shaved, crumbled or grated

[NOTE: Ricotta salata cheese is a crumbly, salty cheese like feta, but drier. If you cannot find it, use feta, but not fresh ricotta.]

In olive oil, heat red pepper and garlic.
Add chopped onions.
Cook over medium-high heat to prevent sticking or burning.
Increase burner to high heat.
Add fresh tomatoes and sauté for 1 minute.
Add sun-dried tomatoes, sauté for 1 minute.
Add arugula and sauté for 1 minute.
Stir in chopped olives.
Lower heat, cover, and let simmer for 5 minutes.
Turn off heat and keep warm until penne pasta is done.
When pasta is just under-done, drain, return to pot.
Toss pasta with sauce over low heat.
Let set a few minutes.
Serve in bowls.
Crumble 1 to 2 Tablespoons of ricotta salata cheese over the top.

Spaghetti Putanesca

[Note: This pasta is made in almost every region of Italy. The name, spaghetti putanesca, *means" whore's spaghetti, supposedly named because it cooks fast, allowing the whore to prepare it "between tricks." Also, the ingredients would likely be found on any Italian kitchen shelf. The whole idea of putanesca is to make do; combining everything, from almonds to zucchini, without fuss or without following a recipe.]*

2 cloves garlic, pressed or finely chopped
½ teaspoon crushed red pepper
½ cup olive oil
¼ lb. oil-cured, sun-dried tomatoes, coarsely chopped (or 1 – 14 oz. can Italian plum tomatoes, drained
18 oil-cured black olives, pitted and coarsely chopped
6 anchovies, rolled with capers
12 basil leaves
1 Tablespoon Italian parsley
1 lb. spaghetti
Freshly grated Parmesan cheese, for use at the table

Over medium-high heat, sauté and garlic and pepper.
Add tomatoes, olives, and anchovies.
Stir briefly.
Add parsley and basil.
Cover and turn off the heat.
Cook pasta.
Before draining pasta, save a few tablespoons of pasta water to add, if necessary, when tossing the pasta with the sauce.
Serve with Parmesan cheese.

Linguine al Vongole (Linguine with White Clam Sauce)

[NOTE: This is the queen of pasta and seafood dishes.]

Olive oil
18 cherrystone clams, shucked with the juice
[NOTE: I buy the clams already shucked in the fish market; now some local grocery stores sell them in a plastic container with the juice.]

25 basil leaves
½ teaspoon dried oregano
¼ cup olive oil
¼ teaspoon crushed red pepper
2 cloves garlic, pressed or minced
1 lb. linguine
Using a strainer, separate the juice from the clams, reserving the juice.
Frisk the clams for pieces of shell and sand.
Option: Filter the clam juice through cheesecloth or muslin.
Wash parsley thoroughly.
If the clams are large, cut them to ¼-inch size, feeling for grit in the process.
Set the clams aside.
Measure 1 cup of the reserved clam juice and place in large bowl.
Add parsley, basil, and oregano.

Heat olive oil with red pepper and garlic until it is sizzling hot.
[NOTE: It is essential for the flavor of this dish that the oil be almost smoking hot when you add the clam juice, as follows.]

Add clam juice/herb mixture.
Stir.
Bring pasta water to a boil and add linguine.
At the same time, add chopped clams to broth.
Increase the heat and bring broth to a boil around the clams.
Turn heat off immediately.
The clams should not boil or they may become tough.
Keep them warm.

[NOTE: In this recipe, the pasta should be significantly underdone, because it needs to absorb a good amount of liquid.]

Cook linguine until three-quarters done or less.
Drain and toss with clam juice mixture.
The absorption will take ten minutes, maybe longer.

[TIP: Stir occasionally so that the pasta absorbs the juice evenly. If there seems to be too much liquid for the pasta to absorb, or if the pasta may be getting cool, warm the liquid to absorb, stirring occasionally over low heat 15 to 30 seconds at a time and again just before serving. This dish is ready to eat only when all the liquid is absorbed.]

———❖———

A Commercial Break to Tell You More about Lucille

Lucille had had a terrible childhood. At six years of age, she worked nine or ten hours a night, opening bushels of clams, slicing cutlets, cleaning and paring vegetables, washing floors, cleaning the refrigerator, stoves, and toilets, but she learned how to cook for a multitude. By the age of fifteen, she cooked as well as her father and mother, and by twenty, she cooked better than her mother, Angie. This, from Reetze (Chapter 16).

Guip De Carlo told me that Sardella's was the hangout of most of the Jersey Mob. Mr. Sardella and his wife were very good to the young up-and-coming mobsters and their families. What he didn't tell me was that the Mob reciprocated magnificently. When Mr. Sardella became ill, he could no longer work. Poor Angie ran the restaurant with young Lucille. The Mob paid Sardella a salary every week and hired and paid extra help for Angie.

When Sardella died, Newark was starting to become a dangerous place to live. The Mob brought Angie to live in Long Branch and rented a lovely apartment on the beach for her and Lucille. Lucille came to work at the Surf, and Angie was treated like a queen until she died at the age of fifty-five.

Pasta con Sarde I (Perciatelli with Sardines & Olives)

[Note: This is a typical Sicilian dish traditionally cooked only on St. Joseph's Day, March 19. Pussy told us that this was a favorite dish of "that Sigie bastard, Lucky Luciano." Lucky for Pussy that Mr. Luciano was living safely away in Naples, so he did not know how Pussy described him. Pussy, incidentally, always called him "Charley Lucky." In fact, the people who knew him intimately never called him Lucky Luciano; they called him Charlie Lucky. Mr. Luciano's real name is Salvatore Lucania.]

½ cup olive oil
½ teaspoon red pepper
1 bulb fennel, cleaned and diced into ½-inch pieces
¼ cup black olives, pitted and chopped
¼ cup Italian parsley, finely chopped
1 lb. spaghetti or perciatelli

In saucepan, heat olive oil and red pepper over high heat.
Add chopped fennel and lower heat to medium-high.
Stir until fennel softens, about 5 minutes.
Add sardines. [Do not expect them to stay whole.]
Sprinkle in the black olives and parsley.
Cover and cover over low heat.
Cook pasta, and drain, reserving some of the water.
Add 1 Tablespoon of pasta water to sauce now and then, if it seems too dry.

Toss pasta with sauce, adding water 1 Tablespoon at a time until the pasta has a slippery coating.

[NOTE: This dish should be moist, but not watery.]

A final word on pasta: There are many shapes of pasta, some never seen in the United States. There are hundreds of sauces. Those from Southern Italy are mostly tomato-based. White cream sauces with vegetables are found in Northern Italy. Lucille knew most of them. They are too numerous to list here, and I would have to write another book, a cookbook, to list them all. Unfortunately, neither time nor health conditions permit.

Meat, Poultry & Fish

On Saturday, we had steak, seldom just broiled, or chicken. There are hundreds of ways to cook chicken. Lucille always cooked fish on Friday.

Steak Oregano

1 stick unsalted butter
Handful of Italian bread crumbs
1 Tablespoon minced garlic
1 Tablespoon oregano
Juice of ½ of a lemon *[The lemon juice makes the mixture smooth.]*

Melt butter and add remaining ingredients.

Spread mixture generously over top of steak, let stand, and then place in pre-heated broiler. Broiling time varies with desired doneness.
Turn steak over and spread the rest of the butter mixture over the steak, return it to the broiler until done.

[NOTE: This butter mixture goes equally well on pork chops. For lamb chops, Lucille spread them lightly with Dijon mustard and broiled them to medium doneness.]

Steak Murphy

[NOTE: I first tasted Steak Murphy at the Surf. Today you will find it in most restaurants, usually made with green and red bell peppers. Lucille used both hot and sweet peppers in vinegar. Her father did not create this dish, but he was the one who made it popular in New Jersey. The name indicates an Irish origin, but not so. It was born in France and called Chicken Morfi. People over the years have bastardized it into Murphy.]

Olive oil
1 small Spanish onion, sliced into 1-inch wide strips
1 small jar sweet peppers in vinegar
2 small hot peppers in vinegar
2 cloves garlic, sliced thin
1 teaspoon capers
1 teaspoon cornstarch
Salt

In frying pan, place 1½ Tablespoons of olive oil.
Sauté onions, garlic, and capers until golden brown. Set aside.
Reserve liquid from peppers.
Cut peppers into 1-inch wide strips.
Cook peppers over medium-high heat until crunchy, about 10 minutes.
To 1 cup of vinegar liquid from peppers, add 1 teaspoon cornstarch.
Place over medium-high heat until slightly thickened.
Add salt to taste.
Add peppers, garlic, onions, and capers.
Add juice of peppers.
Simmer 10 minutes.
Remove and pour over steak, chicken or chops.

Chicken Savoy

[NOTE: This recipe is believed to be the creation of Lucille's father. It was perfected by Stretch, a genius of a chef, and served in his restaurant, the Belmont Café, located on Belmont Avenue in Newark. The name Savoy is lost; perhaps it was named for the Savoy province in Italy. Only a few restaurants serve Chicken Savoy; one place is Giamanos in Bradley Beach, NJ. Peter, the chef there, was one of Lucille's pupils. Giamanos is a wonderful restaurant owned by the Mano family; there you will find many of the Surf's dishes and many of Peter's own specialties. I do not have Peter's recipe for Chicken Savoy; I only remember how Lucille cooked it. Lucille did not use any measuring devices, which makes it difficult to write her recipes. I have cut this one down to serve two.]

1 medium spring chicken, cut into 3-inch pieces
1 cup bread crumbs
1 Tablespoon cheese
1 Tablespoon minced garlic
Pinch of oregano
Salt and pepper to taste
1½ cups red wine vinegar
1½ cups strong black coffee (no sugar)

Mix together bread crumbs, cheese, garlic, and oregano.
Press mixture on chicken, using fingers so mixture adheres to chicken.

Place coated chicken in refrigerator for 10-15 minutes while oven is preheating. *[NOTE: Doing this will help to keep the mixture from falling off the chicken while it is baking. In fact, Lucille always kept the breaded pork chops in the refrigerator overnight.]*

Place chicken in baking pan with enough olive oil to prevent sticking.

Bake chicken until golden brown.

Sprinkle generous amount of coffee/vinegar liquid over chicken, but do not use all of it or the chicken will be soggy.

Place chicken in pan under broiler part of the oven.

Broil until chicken is crispy.

Do not over-broil.

If it burns, throw it out.

[NOTE: I know these ingredients might seem off the wall to most cooks, but this recipe is the only one that I found completely different with chicken. Steaks (never filet mignon) can also be prepared and cooked this way, but never cook fish like this!]

Lucille's fish recipes can be found in most cookbooks. Lucille added some touches to the recipes, however. We had breaded filet of sole, shrimp scampi, shrimp marinara, baked fresh tuna, and lobster tails, all familiar fish and seafood fare.

The following recipe is hard to find. It is made with baccala (dried salted cod) into a sort of fish stew (also a salad recipe that follows the next one). You will find this recipe in Spanish and Portuguese cookbooks.

Baccala (Dried Cod) Stew

1½ lb. dried cod
3 fresh plum tomatoes, peeled and cut into ½-inch strips
1 large Spanish onion, cut into 1-inch strips
2 stalks celery, cut into 1-inch pieces
3 cloves garlic, coarsely chopped
3 large potatoes, peeled and cut into quarters
20 fresh basil leaves
1 small can, black pitted olives, sliced into 4 pieces each
1 small can, green pitted olives, sliced into 4 pieces each
1 large carrot, peeled and cut into ½-inch pieces (optional)
½ cup fish stock (if not available, use bottled clam juice)
3 strips anchovy strips (packed in olive oil) (optional)

Soak dried cod in cold water overnight. It will plump up like fresh cod; if not, change the water and soak in more cold water until it plumps. *[NOTE: Fresh cod can be substituted, but the dried one is worth the effort. It tastes much better in this recipe.]*

When fish is ready, rinse with cold water and pat dry with paper towels.
In medium-sized soup pot, sauté garlic, capers, and anchovies until garlic is yellow in color.
Add tomatoes and cook over medium heat for 10 minutes.
Add fish stock and add water until pot is ¾ full.
Bring to boil.
Add all ingredients except potatoes and cod fish.
Lower heat and cook until carrots and celery are tender, not too soft.
Bring pot to a boil again and add potatoes.
Lower heat and cook for ½ hour.
Add cod and cook until cod flakes.
Cover and let stand 10 minutes.
Serve in large soup bowls.
Garlic bread is a good accompaniment.

Baccala Salad

Treat salted cod the same as for the Baccala Stew.
Simmer cod in water with garlic, onion powder, and about 1
teaspoon black pepper to taste.
When cod flakes, remove, drain, and set it aside to cool.

1 small red onion, sliced and cut into thin strips
1 stalk celery, minced
Small handful pitted black olives

When cod fish has cooled, cut into 1-inch squares.
Place all ingredients in salad bowl.
Sprinkle salt and pepper to taste.
Add ¼ cup olive oil.
Mix well and refrigerate for 30 minutes.
Just before serving, let stand at room temperature.
Add ⅛ cup amount of red wine vinegar, or to taste.
Toss well and serve.

As I said this isn't a cookbook, so let's get back to our story…

Chapter 9

Frank Condi

Big Frank's name was Cocociaro. He liked the name Condi and adopted it. I told him the name suited him, because Condi was the name of the very noble family in Italy and France. One Condi prince was a leader of the early Heugonauts (Protestants) in France. So handsome and refined was he that Queen Catherine de Medici was in love with him.

Frank was not in the least bit vain; in fact, he was quite unaware of how good-looking he was. At that time, he was about forty-six and considered himself a wash-out. When he was sober, he was very shy and quiet; drunk, he was a pain in the ass.

Jo-Jo and I used to tease him unmercifully. He would come into the restaurant, and as soon as we spotted him, we would run and kiss him and tell him that we were in love with him. He would blush and stammer and refuse to look at us. When he was drunk, and we did that, he would growl, "You're full of shit."

In time, he got used to us and would joke back. He loved a good joke, and we saved them up to tell him. He loved Jo-Jo. She was a delight. How he would enjoy it when we did a mock ballet! I would leap into her arms, and she would twirl me around. We would end with the words "foot on the bar" and swing a foot onto the bar in front of him.

One night we told him we were going to take him to a motel and make a sandwich out of him. "Forget about it," he quipped. "I'm a wash-out."

Jo-Jo told him not to worry. "If all else fails, we can tell jokes all night."

Trudy, Frank's wife, was as big as a minute. She barely came to his shoulder in high heels, no less, but she was not afraid of him. One night, not knowing he was a bit tipsy, I gave him the "I love you" routine. He told me I was full of shit.

Trudy turned on him like a wild cat. "Look, you son-of-a-bitch," she screamed. "That's the one who loves you. You better pay attention to that word 'cause that's the only time you will hear it."

It was a wrong move, because that night he was at his fucking worst. He complained about everything. He sent everything back twice, and he even complained about the water. I was in a rage and avoided him.

By closing time, he had mellowed. I had not. When I was ready to leave, I went over to his table and said, "Frank, do me a favor?"

With a gentle smile, he replied, "Of course, sweetheart."

Putting my lips to his ear, I shouted, "Go fuck yourself!"

Now he was sober, indeed. In two years, I had never uttered even a "damn." He ran after me. "What did I do?"

I just drove away. I still wanted to kill him.

The next day was a Sunday, and I arrived at 2 p.m. Frank was waiting at the door. He was very upset and kept asking me what he had done that I, of all people, would curse at him. He told me that Trudy was not speaking to him and that he could not remember being any different than usual.

"Well, Frank, last night you were at your fuckin' worst. You even complained about the water. What do you want me to do about it? I'm not the water commissioner," I hissed at him.

"My God, Frances, you said that word again. You never say that word."

I was ready for him, all right. "Frank, I like that word. It gets rid of my frustrations. From now on, I am going to keep saying that word. Fuck you, Frank."

The look on his face was so comical, I could not help laughing. Frank was relieved. He kept kissing me and asking me to forgive him. Only after I swore on my mother's life that we were friends again did he leave.

From that time on, he had a protective attitude towards me. If Frank was drunk, no one in the restaurant dared complain to me about anything. Trudy thought it was a "scream." One night, the joke was almost tragic.

I first met John Joyce when I rented his house. He was an insidious man. If I had known what I would go through with him, I would have gone to live in the park, before renting his house. John Joyce was the one who brought about the near tragedy.

It was a very slow night, and Frank, Trudy, and I were having drinks at the bar when in walked "Nutsy Fagin," Lucille's name for John Joyce. He was drunk as usual, and I tried to ignore him. In his drunken state, he imagined I was in love with him, so he was going to make me jealous. He asked Trudy to dance. She, of course, told him "I don't dance." This was like putting cat food in front of a cat. He would not take "no" for an answer. So she told him, "Look, I'm Mrs. Frank Condi. Please go away."

I grabbed the dumb bastard by the arm and told him not to push his luck. Frank was in the men's room and had he seen John bothering his wife, it would not go too well for him.

At that moment, Frank returned to the bar. Taking it all in, he gave John one of his blackest looks. Well, John was not that drunk. He dropped my arm like a hot potato and went to the end of the bar.

"Is that bum bothering you?" Frank asked me.

I told him it was just my landlord, drunk as usual, so ignore him.

Frank was not convinced. He was sure that John had said something "nasty" to me. Trudy was worried, because Frank was capable of turning the restaurant into a warehouse when angered.

We managed to calm him down, and he proceeded to get drunk. Frank kept asking me over and over, "Are you sure that guy didn't say anything to you? I'll throw him through the glass window…"

To divert him from this course, I asked him to dance. Onto the dance floor comes that crazy John. He had picked up some bimbo, and he, too, was dancing. Did he quit while he was ahead? No. He made faces at me. Frank, of course, spotted this.

"Did he say something to you? Now, I'm going to throw him through the glass."

He picked up John like a feather, as Trudy screamed. Several men ran over and grabbed John out of Frank's arms. It took six men to hold Frank down. That stupid John just stood there.

Pat Merola threw John out, and it took another hour to calm Frank down. I really could not have cared less what would have happened to John, but we didn't think it was worth Frank going to jail. Besides, I loved John's mother. Poor woman was very ill and did not need the aggravation of him. I continued to protect him for her sake.

One New Year's Eve, I went to work with a very severe cold. How I managed to get through the night, I will never know. New Year's Eve was a nightmare. We served only dinner, and then breakfast at 5 a.m. At about 4 a.m., I looked like death warmed over, and Trudy noticed. "My God, Frank, look at her! I'm afraid she's going to die on us."

I assured him it was just a cold and that I would be okay.

"Are you crazy, Frances? Look at the snow. It must be three feet deep."

Pat Simonetti was singing with the band, and he noticed nothing, not my cold, not Frank's black looks. He just kept singing. Frank stood in front of the band and shouted up to him, "You hard-hearted son-of-a-bitch! Look at that kid. She's sick as a dog. You need the money so bad; I'll pay her salary for the week."

Poor Pat, he would never have let me stay if he knew how sick I was. He was in his own world and too tipsy. "Frank, please, I did not know she was sick. Of course, she can go home."

Trudy was worried about me stepping in the snow. I had no rubber boots (who knew it would snow that night?), and she thought I would get pneumonia, so Frank carried me to his car. The snow was up to his knees, poor man, and he took me home. "Get into some dry clothes," he barked.

As I was changing, I heard this clanking sound coming from the kitchen. There was Frank, boiling water.

"I'm making you a cup of tea. Where is your liquor cabinet? Hot buttered rum is what you need. Fix you up in a jiffy."

He stayed with me until I fell asleep. My own mother could not have been tenderer.

The last time I saw Frank was in Florida. In 1971, he was indicted for something. I forget what it was, and he had just walked out of the courtroom in Freehold, NJ. He was on the lam and had gone into hiding in Florida.

Ft. Monmouth had a package tour to Florida for its employees. I was invited by my friend, Elaine, to go along. Knowing that

Frank was there, I left a message with his friend, Anthony, giving him the name of my hotel. Anthony did not tell him, as he did not know me well, and he feared that Frank might get caught.

Thinking that Frank could not be bothered to look me up, I forgot about it and went to the dog track. We had been swimming during the day and my long hair was not yet dry. Not wanting to delay everyone, I put my hair under this old orange straw hat, big as an umbrella, and off we went.

Going down the escalator at the track, I spotted this tall man going to the exit. His back was turned to me, but I was sure it was Frank. "Frank!" I whispered. "It's me."

The man turns around, and it's Frank. "You som um bitch, I knew it was you under that hat." He grinned.

"Aren't you afraid to be spotted here?" I asked.

He told me he was on the golf course every day. Some police we have! How could they not spot this man, all six feet, four inches of him? He told me that it had been three days before Anthony told him, "Some girl came here looking for you." Anthony was giving him a sly grin; girls were always chasing Frank.

"Describe her," Frank had asked Anthony.

"A dark-haired girl with big boobs and a lovely voice," he replied.

We laughed over that, but it was enough for Frank. He called my hotel and Joanie told him that I am at the dog track so he set out to find me. We had a ball that night. The four of us wined and dined; by at the end of the night, the other three fell in love with him, too.

Frank is gone now. In 1983, he died of a heart attack. He was in prison and was trying to keep in shape by jogging. He was 67 at the time, and I guess the strain killed him.

They say that everyone can be replaced; well, some people are harder to replace than others. As for me, there will never be another Frank Condi. Bless his memory.

Chapter 10

Pat Merola

Pat was the first of my fiancés. Here is how this one started. Pat was a cousin of Morgan, Lucille's then "light o' love," so he became "Cousin Pat."

Both he and I were interested in ancient history. We had many long discussions on the subject, and this formed a bond between us. Also, no one would go to the movies with either of us, because we were both great talkers. We talked in the movies and everywhere else. Hating to go to the movies alone, we had only each other's company.

Frank Sinatra's "The Detective" was playing in Asbury Park. We desperately wanted to see the picture, but Pat had difficulty getting away on a week night, and with me, it was almost impossible to take a day off on the weekend. What to do?

Jessie, a regular at the Surf, was a waitress at the Shadowbrook. She had worked for Pat in the restaurants he had owned before the Surf. She was a friend to all of us and a great gal. Pat and I told her of our problem. Friday was her night off, so she offered to work in my place. I asked Pat's permission (omitting why I wanted the night off), and it was granted.

The other waitresses were told that I had an "important engagement" that night, so Jess was filling in for me. I felt that they would resent my taking Friday off for such a meager reason as a movie.

Pat reasoned that it was nobody's business where he went. "Commit a crime, and the world is made of glass."

Coming out of the movie, we meet Joan Murphy and her husband. Joan worked in the lounge with me, and she lived in Asbury Park, so, of course, she would be the first person we would run into. She pretended to be surprised, but her thoughts were written all over her face.

"Jesus Christ, Pat, we are in the soup now," I said.

He thought I was making too much over it. I knew better. He reasoned that we were liked by everyone, so why should they want to harm us? There is a little envy in all of us, and Pat was considered a great catch.

I, on the other hand, was a married woman respected by all, because I was faithful to my husband. Yet, no matter how much people like you, they can't resist tearing down an idol. All my life, I have been a person that people envied. Why this has been, I do not know, but it is so. It has caused me much grief over the years.

Chef Lucille was possessive of Cousin Pat. She had a field day. Pat laughed over the whole thing; he knew all along about the deception. Many digs were thrown at me, some good-natured, others downright vicious. It unnerved me, and Pat was concerned.

"Look here, Frances, the more you deny it, the more people will believe it. Not only say yes, it's true; exaggerate it." He started the ball rolling by bringing me beautifully wrapped "presents." One was an old sneaker, one a bunch of rusty keys, another, an old broken wristwatch, and so on. No one ever saw me open these "presents," because he told me to open them when I was alone.

The crowning touch was his supposed jealousy of Andy Gerard, who was the perfect foil. He was very shy, especially around women he did not know. The women, in turn, pursued him very aggressively. He was without a doubt the most handsome of all the men who ever entered the Surf. He was a gentleman, and he was rich. When he got to know you and was at ease with you, he was a delight, but just as much of a prankster as Pat Merola was.

I "rescued" Andy one night when a married woman propositioned him right in front of her husband, who left in a rage. This barracuda would not leave him alone. At closing time, I went up to him and said that I would be ready to leave in ten minutes. He caught the drift immediately. "OK, Sweetheart, don't rush." So we left together; the "lady" in question was not about to take me on. He thanked me profusely, and over breakfast I told him about the situation involving Pat and me.

The next day, Pat Simonetti asked me to stop by Chelsea Pool on my way to work. He wanted to see Pat Merola before the restaurant opened. Chelsea Pool was frequented by all the guys. When I saw Pat Merola, he pretended to be very angry because I had had breakfast with Andy the night before. Pat shoved me into the pool. I was furious. How in the world was I going to dry out in time for work? In those days, our uniforms were made of white nylon. You could see through the material, so we wore a full slip. Nylon stockings were a must; pantyhose were not yet in vogue, so most of us wore girdles, as well.

To top it all off, my hair was very long. I had just come from the beauty parlor where I had had my hair all done in elaborate curls set on top of my head.

Now I was a mess. Even if my clothes dried in time, my shoes never would. All I was worried about was my watch. It was a cheap Timex, but it had great sentimental value to me, because it was the one I wore all through my enlistment in the Marines.

I kept screaming over and over again, "You bastard! You ruined my watch! I'll kill you!"

Poor Pat was so upset. I told him that I would not go to work and that, furthermore, I was quitting the job.

"I'll make it up. Please, Frances, if you quit, everyone will hate us."

So, dripping wet, I went with him to Daniel's Uniform Shop, where he told the saleswoman to outfit me from the inside out. He bought me a uniform, shoes, stockings, slip, and girdle. Was I pleased? No!

"What about my hair, you creep? How can I go to work looking like this?"

He then took me to a wig shop and bought me a wig. Was I satisfied? No! I kept screaming to him that my watch was broken. He took me to the local jeweler's for a new watch. In the shop, I embarrassed him further. The jeweler asked him what kind of watch he wanted, a Gruen, a Benrus? They were all beautiful watches with gold, diamonds, you name it. I did not want one of those watches. I wanted my watch repaired.

The jeweler explained that my watch cost only $12.95, and to repair it would cost three times that much.

Poor Pat was desperate. "I don't care if it costs a thousand dollars. Can you repair this one?"

The jeweler agreed to repair the watch.

I was like a mad hornet the whole night. Pat stayed away for two weeks. He finally showed up one night with the repaired watch. I forgave him, and just as I was about to put on my precious watch, he snatched it out of my hand, reached behind the bar for a hammer, and proceeded to smash the watch to bits. "You made such a fuss about this watch; well, here it is."

I started to cry. Poor Pat disintegrated in front of me. "No, Frances, it's only a joke. Here is your watch." That devil had gotten an old Timex, the duplicate of my watch, and smashed it instead. My watch was in his pocket, alongside an eighteen karat gold watch surrounded by diamonds, to make up to me for what I had suffered. I was to consider myself "engaged."

After that, I referred to Pat as my fiancé. This, more than anything, killed the rumors that Pat and I were an "item." The fun went on.

After one of our water fights, Lucille bragged that Pat would never get her. She would get him first. This was tantamount to waving a red flag in a bull's face. Once someone "passed a threat"

to Pat, they were on his "hit list." Lucille was very wary of him. She would not accompany us to breakfast. Pat waited patiently.

The opportunity presented itself by, of all people, the fire department. Every year, in their solicitation of funds for the department, they would go to various restaurants with the fire truck, put on the blinking lights, and then the fire chief would come in for a donation.

When it was our turn for the visit, Pat lost no time using it to his advantage. He told me to make sure Lucille would see him give the fire chief $100. Then I was to tell her that he bribed the fire department to turn the fire hose on her. This, I did, and all hell broke loose.

"Goomara [Godmother], he'll kill me! No one could survive the pressure of that hose," Lucille shouted. She went mad, running out of the place like a demented woman. She ran around the block before we could catch her and calm her down. We feared she would have a heart attack.

Lu was at least a hundred pounds overweight. How puny Pat and skinny me managed to hold her, I'll never know. Eddie Primavera helped us. Pat kept telling her "It's all a joke. Look, Lu, they are gone." But it was a good ten minutes and two brandies later that she finally calmed down. She cursed Pat out (nobody could curse like Lu), but good sport that she was, she forgave him. By the end of the night, she even joined in the laughter. Pat was still bent on drenching her for her threat, and when he finally got even, it was the last of the water fights.

An old friend of mine from high school days loved to visit me at the Surf. Jimmy Bosco was a New York detective by this time. He asked me to not tell anyone that he was "on the job" because he felt it would make people uneasy and I agreed, so I said he was a good friend from the old neighborhood. The gang accepted him as my friend and looked forward to his visits.

Jimmy was a fun-loving person and a good sport. He joined in the merrymaking at our after-work breakfasts.

One particular night, Pat Merola was waiting behind the Surf at closing time to drench Lucille with the garden hose. As fate would have it, he drenched Jimmy instead. Lucille saw him first and hid behind Jimmy, who got all the water.

I was wearing a lovely crepe dress, and it was ruined by the water, as I got hit, too. This pissed me off, so I thought to give it back to Pat. "You did it this time, you silly ass. My friend, Jimmy Bosco, is chief of detectives for New York City, and you just ruined his suit," I shouted.

Pat turned green around the gills. He tried to wipe water off Jimmy's face. Jimmy, in turn, could not stop laughing. He grabbed Pat in a bear hug and thanked him for giving him such as good time. Pat offered to replace the suit. Jimmy brushed this off, saying, "If you buy me breakfast at the famous Ink Well, I'll consider us even." It was love at first sight. The two became fast friends; after all, what could a New York cop do to him?

In the lull, sneaky Pat saw this opportunity and proceeded to drench Lucille as well. At the Ink Well that night, Lucille was shivering, this at the height of summer. We covered her with tablecloths and fed her hot tea. She came down with a bad cold anyway and was sick for three weeks. This sobered Pat, and he never again drenched anyone with water. He used whipped cream instead. Ray Crow quipped, "Pat Merola spends enough money on whipped cream to buy a Rolls Royce."

In or around 1983, Pat went to jail. It was a small charge, and he would be out in eighteen months. Naturally I sent him all kinds of funny letters about how he should ignore all the rumors that I was "unfaithful." I assured him that our "wedding in June would go on" as planned.

Pat's brother, Sally Mo (Mo for Merola) came to the Surf and wanted to meet Pat's fiancée. I proceeded to tell him about the plans for our wedding.

"Oh, it will be the wedding of the century," I gushed. "Helen is the maid of honor. You are the best man. All my waitresses are bridesmaids, and they will wear PF flyers (tennis shoes that we worked in) all studded with sequins. Ray Crow is the little flower boy, and Lucille is the ring bearer. Andy Gerard will give the bride away (serves him right for losing me to Pat); Reetze will play the organ; and Judge Matt (a crooked judge on Pat's payroll) will perform the ceremony. Our honeymoon will be spent on the third floor of the Surf, because Pat Simonetti won't give me any time off. Oh, and last but not least, Pussy himself will drive the getaway car."

Sally thought it was a great joke, and after that always referred to me as "my sister-in-law." He came in one night with two of his henchmen, and I waited on them. He introduced me as his "sister-in-law." Laughing, the men proceeded to act familiar with me. This did not set well with Sally. Looking at them menacingly, he growled, "I said this is my sister-in-law." They paled and behaved very properly after that.

I guess that's how the rumor started that I married Pat Merola; later when I divorced him, he became my "ex-fiancé."

There will never be another one like Pat. We remained close friends until 1989. He succumbed to cancer after a gallant fight. After his passing, a light went out in my life. I will mourn his loss till the day I die. So will the hundreds of people he treated so kindly. He had all the attributes of a prince. "Good night, sweet prince. May flights of angels guide thee to thy rest."

Chapter 11

Sabu

William "Billy" Stefanelli became a master plumber at the age of twenty-one. At nineteen when his father passed away, he was married and his wife was pregnant. At that young age, he became head of his family, his brothers and sister being younger. He had jet black hair and a dark olive complexion. There was not the slightest resemblance between him and the popular movie star, Sabu, the elephant boy. People of Italian descent are great at bestowing nicknames, so because he was dark with the whitest teeth imaginable, they dubbed him Sabu.

Tragedy followed him all his life. He worshipped his wife and daughter and gave them everything their hearts desired. His wife betrayed him by having an affair with his best friend. This unhinged him. He became manic-depressive and was in and out of hospitals the rest of his life.

His parents had a summer home in Long Branch, so after his break-up with his wife, he started a plumbing business there. To be a master plumber at the age of twenty-one was a very rare thing. If he had stuck with it, things might have been different. He was not content with being a plumber; he wanted to be Al Capone. Perhaps he had a subconscious death wish; I don't know, because he was also diabetic and went out of his way to do everything to bring on sickness.

As long as he took his medication, he was normal. A quiet, shy man, so good he was no good. He was one of the softest touches in our crowd. There was nothing dumb about him, but for a street smart person, he was as naïve as a ten-year-old child. He believed and trusted everyone. Some unscrupulous people took advantage of this; in the end, it cost them dearly.

Sabu was in the Surf every night with Barbara, his then light o' love. Barbara was very jealous and possessive. This caused a lot of problems for the waitresses. She was so suspicious of other women; I guess she thought they all wanted to take Sabu away from her. They fought constantly.

One night, the argument became so violent that Sabu struck Barbara. She, too, had a temper and went at him like a wild cat. She was no match for that big ox, and I thought he would kill her. I could not believe that none of the men in the bar came to her rescue. They were too stunned to move quickly.

I guess it was instinct or some deep-down feeling to protect the weak, I don't know, but I flew into a rage and somehow managed to pull him off of her. "You big bully, why don't you pick on someone your own size?" And I slapped him in the face with all my might.

He told me later that I had my fists up like a prize fighter. Anyway, it stopped him cold.

Pat Simonetti took him into the kitchen to cool off, and I took Barbara to the ladies' room to tidy up. She was clinging to me like a baby, and I soothed her. I asked her why she put up with that. I told her that she was a beautiful girl and could have any man of her choice. Dumb me! I didn't know that he was too good for her.

From that night on, I was the only one she trusted. They made up, of course, and we three went to breakfast. I apologized to him for losing my temper and hitting him. He told me that I sounded just like his mother when I screamed at him. He said he and Pat had laughed about it in the kitchen.

I was much smaller than Barbara (though not in the chest) and having referred to me as "someone of your own size" was really comical. It would not have been so comical if he had decided to hit me back. Some angel was looking out for me.

As we were leaving the restaurant, he asked if the slap I gave him entitled him to be one of my fiancés. When they came to dine the following Saturday, I greeted Barbara by saying, "And how is our fiancé tonight?"

That romance was doomed from the start. Barbara wanted marriage. Sabu, on the other hand, was so devastated by his first marriage and the loss of his daughter that he would not chance it. A good marriage would have been the saving of him, because he was at heart a homebody. He knew instinctively that Barbara was not a good risk, but he loved her just the same.

When they broke up, he went to pieces. He drank a lot, stopped taking his medication, neglected his business, and went berserk. He was taken to Marlboro Hospital for the insane. I went to visit him there, and he acted as if I was a life line. I was so sad to see him reduced to this state. My heart went out to him, and I visited him once a week.

There, I met his mother Josephine and his brother Michael. They thanked me profusely for being Billy's friend and insisted that I accompany them to dinner. They had come from Newark to visit. It was long trip and very hard on Josephine. She, too, was diabetic, but in her case it left her blind. She could distinguish between light and dark, but for all practical purposes she was legally blind.

Over dinner, they told me about Sabu's sickness. The worst thing he could do was to drink. He would take his medication and drink, so the sugar in the alcohol would rush to his brain and trigger violence in him.

If a manic-depressive takes his medicine, he can live a normal life. The great playwright, Joshua Logan, was manic. He led a normal life, because Lithium stabilized him.

Sabu was always manic; the diabetes had nothing to do with his periods of violence. Sugar was the catalyst that set off the imbalance in his brain.

Sabu's mother, Josephine, lived with Michael and his wife, but she spent the summers in Long Branch to be with Billy. She was an amazing woman; being blind did not hamper her. She managed to cook and clean the apartment better than most sighted women. We became fast friends, and I promised to look after Sabu during the winter months when she was in Newark.

During those years, she called me "her eyes," and I became a second mother to Sabu. Our crowd wondered why I was the only one who could control Sabu when he was sick. They could see that he was afraid of me. You see, in his head, I was his mother. He did not fear me physically, but he knew I would never hurt him.

Loving his mother the way he did, he would never hurt her, and since I was a substitute mother, the same applied to me.

A manic-depressive is afraid of the world. They think everyone is an enemy out to harm them. This condition in a strong man is dangerous; he will strike to kill in order to protect himself. Every man at heart is a little boy. Sabu was no exception, and even when dangerous, he was still a little boy who looked to his mother for protection. I felt very maternal towards him. I wanted to protect and save him. In that sense, we were made for each other.

So, the legend of Frances grew. When Sabu became violent, he went looking for the people who took advantage of him while he was docile. Up to a point, Nicky Frasco, a good friend, could control him. He protected Sabu, but he was not above taking advantage of him. Nicky was, I believe, a soldier in the Mob, a made man, but a bit lower in the pecking order. The cops referred to him as "Nicky Dirt." Why, I don't know. I just know that he was nice to me, and I liked him.

If Sabu was real bad, only I could calm him down, so they would send for me. I would take him to my house so I could keep an eye on him. In time, he lived more at my house than at his own.

Sabu's first violent incident occurred at the Banjo Palace, one of his hangouts. He was actively involved with an organization called "Ring 4." Retired prize fighters were teaching young kids how to box. The main thing they taught these potential juvenile delinquents was sportsmanship. The organization was always trying to raise money to send the kids to camp, maintain a clubhouse, buy equipment, and so on. Sabu was one of their main boosters.

That night, he was hanging a poster for the club, when a customer at the bar advised him to hang it on the opposite wall for better viewing. Sabu went berserk. Not knowing what to do, the bartender called the Surf. We were in the middle of the Saturday night rush hour, but Pat Simonetti told me to go and see what I could do to help them at the Banjo.

What happened next was straight out of a scene in a Grade B movie. There was Sabu with a three-day-old growth of beard, his eyes looking like two cherries in a glass of milk, and he holding a gun at this poor young guy's temple. The rest of the people were frozen stiff with terror. I ran in shouting, "So, here you are, you son-of-a-bitch! I've been waiting for you for one hour to take me to breakfast."

He gave me this hang-dog look and mumbled, "I didn't know that."

He was still holding the gun, and I'm praying to all the saints to aid me. "What are you doing? He's a friend of mine."

Handing me the gun and hanging his head in shame, Sabu answered, "Gee, Frannie, I didn't know that."

You could hear the sighs of relief all throughout the room. "I'll give you five minutes to make yourself presentable, and then with or without you, I'm going to breakfast."

Sabu meekly went to the men's room. The kid whose life was threatened was sobbing and kissing my hands. "Lady, I don't know where you came from, but God bless you."

I knew I had to scold Sabu like his mother to distract him. It worked every time.

The next incident began the following week. Livia, one of the cocktail waitresses, and I are going to breakfast at the Ink Well when I spot Sabu's car in front of Linda's Cliff House. Only five hours earlier, I had given him enough Thorazine to put an elephant to sleep for a week. I couldn't believe my eyes. Here we go again, gang; another fuckin' night with Sabu.

He was at the bar with a screwdriver in front of him. Now, I was pissed. Alcohol in his present state was bad, but orange juice was a disaster. Anything could trigger his violent temper.

"What are you doing here?" I shouted at him. "Is that a screwdriver you're drinking, you dumb bastard?"

Turning to Frankie Count, the bartender, I demanded that he take the drink away from Sabu.

"Are you crazy? You take it away from him!"

It was the worst thing he could have said. Now, Sabu thought he had an ally to help him defy his "mother." I threw the drink in his face and told him that now he could go home with Frankie and never come to my house again.

He appealed to Livia for aid. "Gee, what did I do? She is always in a bad mood. Please talk to her."

Grabbing Sabu's arm, she followed behind me, soothingly telling him, "It's all right. She doesn't mean it. Let's go get something to eat."

Livia was one gutsy lady. She was never frightened of Sabu. We called her "Mighty Mite." Five feet nothing, weighing all of a hundred pounds, she stood up to anyone.

This pattern was to continue on and off for the next thirty years. The sad part is it never needed to have happened. We saw at least fifty doctors, in an out of several hospitals, and not one of them prescribed Lithium to Sabu. I blame myself for not reading up on it and asking questions. With the proper medication, Sabu would have led a normal life, like the thousands of manic-depressives in the country are living to this present day.

Because Josephine was helpless in Newark, I took over signing him in and out of hospitals, because I had power of attorney and posed as Sabu's sister.

No blood brother could have been to me what he was—a big teddy bear. When he was well, as gentle as a kitten, there wasn't a malicious bone in his body. You could have searched the world over and never have found a more loyal friend. Too bad he befriended those who were not as loyal as he was. It was to be his downfall.

In 1972, we lost Josephine. She was in a great deal of pain and refused to give into it. She told me she could not die right then, as she was worried about what would happen to Billy. I assured her that I would look after him for as long as I lived. Smiling sadly, she asked "Would you put your hand on the cross (the crucifix hanging over her bed) for me?"

I put my hand on the cross, and I have been on that cross ever since. When Josephine died, I continued to call Sabu, Billy.

Billy took his mother's death very badly. He neglected himself and ended up at Marlboro Hospital. Though he was far from well, they released him into my custody, and I took him home.

He got into the wrong company (a disease with him), and I stood by helplessly. Ironically, it was during his "being good to please Frannie" stage that disaster fell.

After I gave him enough Thorazine for the night, I went to bed. About 3 a.m., the phone rang. We picked it up at the same time.

"Hello, Sabu? This is John."

"Yeah, John, what's up?"

"We can't open the safe. Can you help us out?"

"Sure, John, I'll get dressed and be right over."

In my dining room was his box of plumbing tools. He was picking them up as I entered the room. "Where are you going, Billy?"

"I'm going to help John Petrone. He's in trouble."

Can you believe that?

"Billy, if you leave this dining room, you will go straight to jail."

And that's just where he went. Do you think the three years he served for that fiasco taught him a lesson? No, indeed; he was on parole for one year, when Nicky Frasco needed help. Nicky at least really liked Billy. He was patient and kind with him, especially when he was sick.

Nick was never in trouble and had never been arrested. Why he went into this hair-brained scheme, I will never figure out. This wealthy woman offered him a few thousand dollars to burn her house. He offered Billy three thousand dollars to set it on fire. Now, Billy was doing well in the plumbing business. He owned a boarding house and was not desperate for three thousand dollars, so would he take the chance? To help his friend, that's why.

I tried to reason with him. Using his standards, I asked, "What the hell do you know about arson? You have been a thief all your life!"

He assured me that it was a "piece of cake." I told him that if he needed three thousand dollars so badly, why, I'd give it to him. He pretended to agree with me, but he winked at Nick.

"Go ahead," I told him, "but as soon as you leave this house, you'll be on your way to jail."

I wish I could say that I was wrong, but I wasn't. He got fifteen years in prison. Nicky got twenty. The woman who wanted her house burned, why, she got six months. Her husband claimed no knowledge of the crime. He got three hundred and fifty thousand dollars. When his wife got out of jail (after serving only four months), they retired and went to live in Florida. God bless America.

After serving seven years in prison, Billy came home in 1990. In 1998, he had a triple bypass. He was very frightened at the mere thought of this operation, but I told him that no one seemed to die on the table, not even ninety-year-olds. It was after the surgery that he had to watch himself. He, of course, ignored my advice. He kept on smoking and helping his friends with plumbing work.

Shortly after the operation, Billy died. This man was my best friend. He was the best man at my second wedding. My Raymond loved him, too. I knew that if anything happened to me, Billy would take care of my children and my Raymond.

Chapter 12

Johnny Maggio

I loved at first sight the ever-cheerful little man, Johnny Maggio. He looked like the classic picture of a leprechaun, *sans* cap and beard. He was the eternal "cockeyed optimist." Though down on his luck, he was not in the least bit gloomy.

Sabu told me that his friend Johnny Maggio thought he knew me from somewhere. I paid no attention to this remark. Coming from New York, the only people I knew from Jersey were my family. Sabu insisted that it must be so, because his friend "never forgot a face."

When he introduced me to Johnny, I told him that I was from New York and he must have me confused with someone else. Maggio told me that he, too, was from New York. After comparing notes, we found that we both came from the Bronx, although he was now living in New Jersey. John was at least ten years older than I, so attending school was out.

"Did you ever live in Harlem?" he asked.

"I lived there till 1960, and then I came here to Jersey." My Aunt Sophie lived on 121st Street and Pleasant Avenue in Harlem.

Her husband, my Uncle Louie, had a printing store on 116th Street. Perhaps he saw me there.

"Yes, that's it! I had a grocery store on Pleasant Avenue between 120th and 121st Streets. Maybe you shopped there?"

I did not remember him from Adam, but to please him I said I did. For John, this formed a bond between us. The little man went on to tell me how at one time he was a "big man" in Harlem. Drink was his downfall, however, and he was in some trouble in New York, so he came to the Jersey shore. He seemed quite content to eke out a living there. Of course, he always needed something— money, my car, my influence with Sabu, and so on. I was not put out by this, because if John "made a score" he shared his good fortune.

His constant companions were Greg Jarvis and Skippy's son, Jimmy. Greg was a bartender, Jimmy a plumber, and the two worked constantly; yet, for some reason or other, they were usually broke. Maggio, on the other hand, never worked but he was no worse off than the other two. Many a morning, they would arrive at my door and tell me "the diner was closed." Sheer nonsense. The diners all over town stayed open twenty-four hours. They were broke and hungry, so I fed them. They were a gay Bohemian lot, and I looked forward to their company.

One night after closing the Surf, Livia and I went to the Ink Well for breakfast. There, parked in the middle of the street, engine running, was Lucille's car. No one seemed to be in it. I was alarmed, but Livia was laughing.

"For God's sake, Lucille must be in trouble. What are you laughing at?"

"That's not Lucille," Livia replied. "She is selling the car to Maggio. He's drunk again, and he left it there. But it's still in Lucille's name; if the cops come, she will get a summons."

We go to the car, and there is Maggio, slumped over the seat. It looked like he was wrestling with an octopus. "Jesus Christ, it's an opium pipe. We've got to get the car out of here."

"Maggio, wake up! Move over. We've get out of here."

The little bastard was zonked. "Frances, leave me alone. I want to die."

"You'll die, you son-of-a-bitch, but not in Lucille's car."

With Livia's help, I shoved him over to the passenger's side and drove to my house. Livia followed in my car.

Maggio could not have weighed more than a hundred and thirty-five pounds, but he was dead weight. We could not get him out of the car. We managed to get the hookah pipe out of his arms, and so we left him there to sleep it off. I didn't know what to do with the damned pipe. Taking it into the house was out of the question, because my children might find it. I called Sabu, and he got rid of it.

After telling him that I never wanted to see him or Maggio again in my life, I went to bed. Around noon, I went out to check on Maggio, and the car was gone. Since I had the keys, I figured he had hot-wired the car and driven off. This was not the case at all. In my agitated state of mind, I had parked the car the wrong way on the street. The cops found it and had it towed away with the sleeping Maggio inside.

Nothing happened to Maggio (even the cops liked him), but Lucille was hit with a summons and the cost of towing the car. For two days, the guys kept Maggio hidden or Lucille would have killed him. I felt guilty because I was the one who had parked the lousy car. To keep in my good graces, Sabu paid all the costs; nevertheless, it was a whole month before I could speak to either one of them.

Lucille sold the car to someone else, and Maggio was out of wheels. I knew better than to lend him my car. His license was always suspended for driving under the influence of liquor. Only Sabu was stupid enough to lend him a car.

During this time, Pussy went into the hospital for a hemorrhoid operation. I sent him a telegram reading, "Boss, I always knew you would get it in the end." His reply was a drawing of a black hand dripping blood with the message "Get out of town" written on the back. We had a good laugh over this and were friends again.

Maggio lost no time in asking me to lend him my daughter's bicycle so he could visit Pussy in the hospital. Dope that I was, I gave him the $150 bike, and that was the last I saw of him for two weeks.

When I finally tracked him down, he told me that the bike had been stolen in the hospital parking lot. My poor daughter paid for that bike herself with prize money she earned selling the most candy for her school. We got her another bike, but she held it against me. I vowed to get even with Maggio. A few months later, I got my chance.

He asked me if I knew anyone who would buy a child's gold charm bracelet. He only wanted a hundred dollars for it, but it was worth much more. It was stolen, of course, so I sold it to Sabu for one hundred and fifty dollars (the price of the lost bike).

When Maggio came to ask for the money, I told him he owed me fifty dollars, since he wanted a hundred dollars for the bracelet, and my daughter's bike had cost fifty dollars more. I kept the hundred dollars and decided to make fifty dollars' profit for my trouble.

Vinnie thought this was poetic justice when Maggio complained to him, "I'm always getting robbed." In one blow, I got even with Maggio (he obviously had sold the bike) and Sabu for not putting him in his place for this affront. The two took it good-naturedly, and life went on as usual.

The meeting between Maggio and Jimmy Bosco is a classic. Jimmy had come to spend the weekend at my mother's house, so he was visiting with me at work. Maggio was staring at us so intently that Jimmy began to feel uncomfortable. He asked who the little guy was, and I assured him that he was harmless. Perhaps Maggio thought that Jimmy was bothering me. Maggio was capable of causing a commotion, so I motioned for him to join us. "It's OK, Madge, this is one of my ex-fiancés, Jimmy Bosco," I tossed at him.

"Don't I know you from some place? You look familiar to me," said Maggio.

"Yes," Jimmy replied, "so do you."

I thought Jimmy was putting him on.

"Do you come from Harlem?"

"No, the Bronx, but my first job was in Harlem. I used to hang around in the Bronx. I think I met you at the Irish Center."

Back and forth it went. "Do you know so-and-so?"

"You met me in Harlem," Jimmy said.

"Are you sure?"

"Oh, yes, quite sure. I met you in front of your store on Pleasant Avenue; the store with one can of olive oil in the window. Do you remember?"

Maggio was thinking real hard. "I sold the store twenty years ago. Are you sure you met me there?"

"If I remember, the store was a front. You were booking numbers there. Now do you know me?"

Maggio protested, telling Jimmy the store was legitimate.

"Aren't you the guy who was always driving around without a license?" Jimmy asked.

"Yes, that's me. How did you know?"

"Well, I was working my first job in Harlem. You were speeding. I chased you, and you offered me a bribe, so I bagged you. Now do you remember me?"

I expected Maggio to run out of the place, but he never did the things you expected. Grinning like a baboon, he shook Jimmy's hand and said, "You son-of-a-gun, was that you?"

I must have had a dumb look on my face, so Maggio explained it all to me. "You see, Frannie, in those days I was a big bookmaker. I was forever having my license revoked. The cops knew this, so every time they needed money they would wait for me to drive my car. They would stop me and ask for my license. I would give them a hundred dollars, and they would let me go. This was the first honest cop I met there, so instead of taking my money, he arrested me."

"You're not mad?" I asked.

"Hell, no. That was twenty years ago. All water under the bridge." That was Maggio.

A little while before Pat Simonetti sold the Surf, we got a busboy for the first and last time. Stanley was a student from Monmouth College studying psychology. He had first worked at the Harbor Island Spa, where the money was not good enough to pay his tuition, so good-hearted Pat offered him a job.

Stanley was a nice kid and a good worker. He seemed to know all "our Jews," our steady customers who also frequented the spa. Someone bought him a drink, and apparently he liked it, because he kept taking drinks from the bus trays. An hour before closing, he passed out like a light.

Pat was singing with the band; from the stage, he noticed Stanley's condition and proceeded to tell his customers, "You people think that's funny? You ruined me. The first time I get a busboy, you get him drunk."

Rita, the head waitress, asked me what we should do with him.

"Throw him in the ocean. That'll sober him up."

Poor, refined Rita. She was about to cry.

"I know where he lives," I said, "so I'll ask the guys to put the son-of-a-bitch in my car, and I'll take him home."

As we were carrying him out, Maggio arrived, drunk as usual. "Frannie, is that the waiter? He's so fuckin' drunk."

"Drunk? You think he's drunk? I think he's dead."

Walking over to take a closer look and smelling him in the bargain, he turned to me, shaking his head. "Frannie, so help me God, I'll never take another drink in my life. I never knew anyone could be so fuckin' drunk."

If only he meant it, it would have saved him three years of his life. No one could have prevented what happened next.

Most people would not believe the event that sent Maggio to jail. He was very drunk when he wandered into Linda's Cliff House, a local bar, that fatal night. The place was crowded, so whatever possessed him to hold up the place, I'll never know. That night he had two thousand dollars in his pocket; he certainly didn't need money. He was not by any stretch of the imagination a "hold-up" man. In his pocket was a toy gun. Even the cops knew that this was his way of playing a joke. To them, he was a harmless drunk. They did not want to arrest him, but Mr. Lombardi, the owner of the bar, pressed charges.

I was talking to Andy Gerard at the Surf bar, when Sabu rushed in to tell me the news. I started crying, "My God, Andy, the poor little guy! He has a wife and small kids. What's going to happen to him?" I sobbed.

Andy asked Sabu who Maggio was, and Sabu told him the story.

"Let's go see what we can do," said Andy. "Don't cry, Frannie. It will be all right."

It wasn't. Andy offered Mr. Lombardi five thousand dollars to drop the charges. He refused. Maggio went to jail for three years. What a farce! God bless, Andy. I can't think of any straight guy doing that for a stranger. Maybe a Howard Hughes, but then again, not likely.

In jail, Maggio did "good time." This man refused to be undaunted. He cheered up the other inmates. While he was there, the time passed more quickly for them. When his time was up, all the prisoners (and most of the guards) chipped in and bought him a farewell gift—a ring shaped like a gold nugget. I believe that this was a rare thing. I doubt that you would find a similar story even in the Guinness Book of World Records.

Chapter 13

Vinnie

Vinnie had been working for Lionel Trains in Newark. It seems he had made a mess out of his life. Gambling, drinking, and debts cost him a marriage. He found happiness with his second wife, Patti, a truly beautiful person. He came to Long Branch to start a new life. In this, he succeeded. He built a lovely home and had three wonderful children. He stopped gambling, carousing, and became an exemplary husband and father. We were fortunate that his transition landed him at the Surf.

Vinnie was born to be a bartender. He had a phenomenal memory for faces. If a person came into the bar just once and then returned a year later, he would remember not only the person's name, but also what he drank. He could handle the whole bar, which seated at least forty people, plus the service end, where the waitresses came for the drinks for the dining room customers.

He constantly amazed me. I would go to the bar and order ten drinks (which I had written down). When I went for the second round, he had memorized the order. I never had to repeat the order.

He liked all of his customers and was a pseudo-father confessor. He holds many secrets.

He pretended to be money hungry for tips, but he was no worse than the rest of us. He made a game out of "milking tips" from the customers. He was my confidant. He knew more about me than anyone. We had our little differences now and then, but it never destroyed our strong friendship.

I can't pinpoint the exact night I met Vinnie. I think he came during the winter, and in the early days I was not there the winter months, because I would go to wherever my husband was stationed. I do remember that Vinnie was already established by the time I came back in the summer.

The third year I was working at the Surf, my husband was stationed in Beaufort, South Carolina. It was a lovely place, and I was quite happy there, but of course I preferred being at home in New Jersey with my family, if only for the summer months. I poked fun good-naturedly at South Carolina, telling one and all that it was the "land that time for got."

Vinnie, always thinking, remarked, "It would be a good place to hide out."

During that summer, Pussy was in some sort of trouble with the law, and I told him, "If you have to go on the lam, go to Beaufort. The Angel Gabriel would not find you there." We had a good laugh and forgot about it, or so I thought.

Joey Scotti, one of our regulars, heard my remark and asked me about Beaufort. I told him that it was hick town, but I liked it. I had a lovely three-bedroom Capehart home there, and I liked the climate.

Well, lo and behold, in October of that year, I got a call from Joey.

"Where are you?" I thought he was in Newark or Long Branch.

"Orangeburg. How far away am I from Beaufort?"

He told me he was thinking of paying me a visit. I figured he was driving to Florida and decided to stop in to see me. Well, my friends, he was on the lam and "visited" me for three-and-a-half months! I could never prove it, but I strongly suspect that the ever-sympathetic Vinnie put the thought in Joey's head to visit me. He did a lot of little things like that to me, but it was all in good fun, and I never minded. I played a few tricks on him, too, but when push came to shove, we were solidly behind each other.

Frank Condi was one of Vinnie's nemeses. He loved Vinnie, but when he got drunk he imagined that Vinnie was padding his bar bill. Frank would come in and during the course of the night order drinks for all and sundry. When he was ready to leave (a little drunk), he would ask for his bill. Seeing all the drinks there, he would go to the bar and yell at Vinnie, "You bald-headed bastard! How could I have drunk this much?"

Vinnie was, by no means, bald. He had a just little bald spot on the back of his head. To his credit, he stood his ground. He was terrified of Frank (and who wasn't?) but he tried to calm him down. He could have complained to Pat or even to Pussy, but he did not, and so it went week after week. One night, it got to me.

At the end of that Saturday night, Frank asked me for his tab. Same routine, number five, he goes over to Vinnie, accusing him again. I told him that if Vinnie was stealing from him, he would not have rung up the drinks, since they were all on his bar bill. I asked him if he thought Pat Simonetti was stealing from him, since the only one who would benefit from a padded check would have been Pat.

He stormed out of the place, but he must have been thinking about it. The next day was a Sunday, and in came Frank before the restaurant opened. Vinnie thought he was coming to hit him; instead, in a maudlin voice, he says, "Vinnie, I done it again. I'm sorry. Please don't mind me."

Poor Vinnie, he was telling him that it was all right and he understood. Did it stop? No! Frank continued to harass Vinnie till the day we closed. I don't know how he stood it. Time and time again he was in hot water, and he was always completely innocent. Like the Sabu incident.

Sabu was at the bar talking to Vinnie, and Frank was at a nearby table. Vinnie asked Sabu for a loan of $300. Frank, overhearing this, went to the bar and shouted to Vinnie, "You bald-headed bastard, I helped you. I did not charge you interest, and now you go to him?"

Turning to Sabu, he put his finger on his nose and whispered, "And, you, don't you do a fuckin' thing in this town without telling me."

Frank thought Sabu was in the Shylock business and was taking away from him. Sabu never said a word, but Vinnie stood up to Frank and told him that Sabu was innocent, that it was a personal loan from a friend, with no interest involved. That took great courage on his part. Vinnie weighed maybe 135 pounds, and Frank was no one to mess with when angry. You could reason with him when he was calm, but aroused, he was a mad dog. The outcome was that Frank respected Vinnie all the more, and Sabu would have died for him.

My first falling out with Vinnie, which lasted one night, came about when he caused me to enter a marathon dance. One of the regulars loved to dance. He could not dance to save his soul. He was an arm pumper, and he stepped on your feet. What the hell! One dance would not kill me, so I got up to dance with him. That was the longest dance in history. The band (Nicky Don) kept playing song after song with no break, not even half an hour.

I was in agony. The band just kept playing. I looked over to Vinnie, and he was laughing like a hyena, enjoying my misery. It did not take a genius to figure it out. He told Nicky to keep on playing, and, jerk that I was; I kept on dancing.

In a fury, I picked up a drink and threw it in Vinnie's face, breaking the glass and messing up his station, and I stormed out.

My dancing partner did not know what had happened. Suffice it to say, I never saw him again.

The next day, I saw the humor in it and forgave Vinnie. I forgave him, but I did not forget. What's good for the goose is good for the gander. I waited for my opportunity to get back at him. It came very soon.

"Lucky" Lavoi was a good friend to all, but he could be a bad enemy. He was from "Hell's kitchen." A gentle giant, loyal to his friends; your troubles were his troubles. The only difference between him and Sabu was that Sabu had to be in his violent period to come to your defense. Sabu went out of his way to avoid trouble when he was well. Lucky, if he thought a friend was being harassed, would go against God Himself. And Lucky was not insane. So...

I told Lucky in a half-joking way that Vinnie was always abusing me. He asked me in what way. "Well, he blames me for his mistakes in the drink orders (Vinnie never made a mistake). He thinks he is funny, but he costs me money." And whatever other lies I could think of. Sabu was at the bar taking it all in. Lucky half believed me; he too loved Vinnie. So he watched and waited.

Reetze, one of the really big spenders, was having dinner and to spite Vinnie, I told him to have his drinks in the dining room since the bar was full. Vinnie would have thrown two people off their stools to have Reetze at the bar, and not only for the big tip. Reetze was very witty and a real pussycat.

So, Vinnie was fuming. "Okay for you, Frances. I'll get even," he hollered over at me. This went all over Reetze's head, but he asked me what Vinnie meant.

"Oh, he is always abusing me. He is jealous because my tips are bigger than his." This was another lie. Vinnie earned three times the amount that I did, and Reetze knew it.

"OK. Get his name and address," said Reetze jokingly. That was enough for Lucky.

He now believed me, and he leaned over the bar and threatened Vinnie in some way. Pat calmed him down, and Reetze left. We were not concerned. Lucky was no killer.

Sabu was something else. He was now out of his docile period (I did not know it), and he remembered my saying that Vinnie abused me. Remember in Sabu's head I was his mother.

I was in the kitchen when Sabu sprang. It took six people to subdue him. Pat talked Maggio into taking Sabu out of the bar. I missed the whole thing. I came and out Vinnie was really mad.

"Goddamn it, Frances, watch what you tell these guys."

I felt so bad. I would never have sicced Sabu on anybody, let alone Vinnie. I straightened out with Lucky and Sabu, and I never did it again. The battle of wits still went on, and we all enjoyed it.

The one who should be writing this book is Vinnie; not only does he have a better memory, but he witnessed much more than I did; and last but not least, he was a better storyteller than I am. Maybe I can interest him in writing *Hello, Soif II*. I doubt it. Vinnie's biggest fault was that outside of bar work, he was lazy.

Vinnie stayed with the Surf till it burned down in 1981. Then he came to work at the North Shore Inn, and we were reunited again. My friend, Marie Gazzola, was part owner of the place, and I worked for her. It was a nice place, and we even had Pat a few years with us, but it was not the same.

When the North Shore Inn was sold, I went to Sirianni's and was reunited with Vinnie for the last time. I continue do see him after I left there for my job in New York.

In 1989, he left for Florida. I hope to go visit there one day. If not, I hope that he and I will be reunited in that "great cocktail lounge in the sky" someday. I can't think of anyone I would rather spend eternity with than Vinnie.

Chapter 14

Louie Ross

Before I really got to know Louie, I believed everything he said. He could say the most outrageous things, the most blatant lies with a straight face. I would ask what happened to so and so, and he would say, "Oh, he died." Pussy would do the same thing, but we never believed him. He was known as a practical joker.

I asked Louie if his name was Ross; he surely did not look like a Ross. Pat told me, "He stole his brother's name. It was resented, so now he is Mr. L. Ross of Las Vegas."

In the old days (way before the Landmark or the Surf), he was Butch's partner, whatever the hell that meant. Butch told me that at one time they were both picked up by the cops and put in a jail cell. The cell was so dirty that Louie "stood up for three days." Yes, that was Louie, immaculate!

I was having one of my usual arguments with my mother, and I was in a foul mood.

Louie and Pat Simonetti were going to the movies. They asked me if I had seen the picture that was playing. "The last movie I saw was 'Ben Hur' with Ramon Navarro and Francis X. Bushman," I snarled at Pat. He, of course, laughed.

Louie, however, saw that something was wrong. "What is it, Frances? You're not yourself tonight."

I didn't want to tell him my troubles but I was afraid he would think one of my customers was bothering me, so I said, "God help me, Louie, but that SOB is going to drive me to the insane asylum."

He grabbed my hands and in his soft, lilting voice, he said, "Frances, what are you worrying about? Five hundred dollars takes care of the job. Do you want him standing up or lying down?"

Horrified, I squealed, "Louie, I'm talking about my mother!"

He turned beet red. "Oh, your *mother*. Well, from your mother, you have to take shit. You gotta have respect."

This cracked me up, and my humor was restored.

In 1963, Louie was down on his luck, so Pat gave him a job. He was to seat the people as they came in. Helen was schooling him. "Now Louie, as the people come in, you greet them and ask if they are having dinner or cocktails. If it's dinner, you seat them in the dining room; if it's cocktails, you take them to the lounge."

I could see that the perfectionist Helen had some misgivings. I pointed out that if anyone looked the part of a host or maitre d', it was Louie.

"What if he 'dees, doze, and dems' our Jews? They will walk out."

I did not agree. Our Jewish clientele were not snobs, and they were all blessed with a sense of humor. They were used to the unorthodox way Pat ran the restaurant. I, for one, thought they would love Louie, as we all did. Besides, most of them had seen Louie, and some even knew him well.

We started him out on a week night, what with weekends being so busy. The night passed without a snag, and Louie seemed to be enjoying himself.

Saturday came, and Pat as usual was singing with the band. Louie was taking his place as host. Four strangers came in dressed in formal clothes. Louis approached them. "Youse want a menu or what?" he sneered.

The people were perplexed, so he continued, "Youse wanna eat or drink?"

Pat was taking in the whole thing from the stage. "'Youse want a menu or what?' What else would they want, you son-of-a-bitch!" he yelled.

Helen rushed over to rescue these poor souls. She assured them that Louie was only filling in. It was too much for her; her gallbladder was acting up, and she went home in agony.

Pat was not angry; he thought the whole thing was funny; so did the rest of the customers. For me, it was a delight watching Louie. As the people came in, he would eye them up and down and, with an expression of utter disdain, he would motion with his head the direction they should go.

Vinnie kept laughing. "It looks like he is taking them for their last ride." That's just what it looked like.

Helen, thank God, was spared the last "goof up." I was at the table reserved for the crew, grabbing a bite to eat, when Louie hollered from the back of the lounge. "Frances, tree people came in. I trew them in the back." The whole place broke up.

Phil Islin, the owner of the Jets and Monmouth Park, was a regular and a friend of Pat's. He called me over and said, "You sure can count on good old Pat for a million laughs."

He and all the others thought the whole thing was put on. Louie was a great success. He never smiled and never engaged in light talk with the customers, and so he set a standard. The slightest sign of recognition from Louie established you as an "in person." I started calling him Albert.

"Who dat?" he questioned.

"Why, Louie, that is the name of the maitre d' at Maxim's in Paris."

The only one who appreciated my quip was that splendid specimen of manhood, Walter Reed, the owner of the Walter Reed chain of theatres. God, he was gorgeous! And the nicest, friendliest man you could wish for. He was a jet setter and quite familiar with Maxim's.

"Do you know Albert, Frances?" Walter smiled.

I told him that I had never met the man, only read about him. He in turn told me that Albert was there in his father's time, and it was his father who told him about the legend of Albert.

Pretty soon, everyone was calling him Louie Albert. This ruffled Louie's feathers and at long last, he asked, "Who is this friggin' Albert?"

So I told him the following story: "The people who patronized Maxim's were very snobbish. Among them were dukes, marquis, barons, the multi-rich, celebrities, and so on. Now Albert was not impressed by anyone. He was a little warm only to the people he really liked. If the person was an impoverished count, and he liked him, he extended himself. If the person he didn't care for was the Queen of England, he was his cold, haughty self. It became ridiculous. Albert's greeting made or broke one's standing in European society, so naturally those people went out of their way to curry favor with him."

Louie could not understand how Albert got away with this. Why, in America, he would have been fired. So, I went on to explain that since Albert was a bigger snob than all the rest of them put together, he was able to treat them exactly as he pleased. He played on people's insecurity.

"Oh, a super con man." That was our Louie.

He soon tired of being host and returned to being just one of Pat's cronies, but we still used him from time to time. The best Louie Ross story, as far as I am concerned, is this one.

Vinnie's wife, Patti, was the one who handled our few difficult customers. She could charm a bird from a tree. She was so filled with human kindness that the crankiest bastards could not bear to abuse her. She never lost her cool, so on that night when she told me, "I can't go near that table again. Please see what that obnoxious man wants," I was amazed.

The table she was referring to was occupied by Lew Harvey and his guests. Lew was a perfect gentleman. He could be a little sarcastic at times, but never rude or abusive. That night, he was dining family style; the customers served themselves. There were large platters of roast beef, chicken Marsala, pasta, mashed potatoes, and three or four vegetables.

I went to the table, and one of the party said, "I want the boss." Helen came over to the table to see what the trouble was. "I'm the head waitress, sir. May I help you?" she said in her best school teacher manner.

"I don't want you. I want the boss!" he bellowed.

She was not about to tell him that the boss was on the stage singing with the band. So she went over to Louie. "Louie, will you please go over there and play boss and see what that man wants?"

I couldn't wait to see how this played out. Louie went over to the table. "What is it?" he snarled.

"We ordered family style. There's no gravy for the roast beef."

Louie turned and said with his lazy drawl, "Where is it?"

There, in a gleaming gravy boat was the *au jus.* I pointed to it.

"I don't want that. I want brown gravy." By now, the man was almost hysterical. He was a bit tipsy, and I thought he was going to create a scene. "Louie, they ordered *au jus*, not brown gravy."

The man glared at me, "You are not my waitress."

Louie was prepared for him. He looked at me and snarled, "What's wrong with youse? Youse should have trew it on before youse brung it out."

Stone silence. Lew Harvey was grinning from ear to ear. The complaining man? He turned to Louie, all smiles now. "Hey, you're all right."

He thought Louie was putting him on.

I asked Louie what he would have done if the man was not satisfied with his handling of the matter. Shaking his head sadly at my lack of understanding, he said, "I would have told youse that youse were fired."

The man was a bloody genius. Of course, by firing me, the customer would have felt sorry for me (unless he was a vicious bastard) and would have gone out of his way to be nicer. Louie opened a door for us. From that night on (until the people got wise), we played boss for one another and fired each other left and right.

Shortly after Pat sold the Surf in 1968, Louie left for Florida. I lost contact with him. Now and then, we would hear about him from Charlie Pine, one of our bartenders, who also left for Florida. I can't be sure what year it was, but it was sometime in the 1970s that Vinnie told me that Louie had died. We both cried over the news.

Vinnie was such a soft-hearted person under that hard veneer he hid behind. Coming from Newark, Vinnie knew all the gang well; Louie was one of his favorites. He will live on in these pages and in my heart, as well.

Chapter 15

"P.D."

P.D.'s given name was Pat. What his surname was I never knew. He was a natty little man with the disposition of a saint. He had a bar in Newark called The Twilight Zone, very *a propos*; his whole life was spent in the twilight zone. He resembled Milburn Stone, the actor who played Doc on the TV series, "Gunsmoke." To this delightful character, life was one big joke.

How P.D. loved the ladies, one in particular. Roma was a regular customer at the Surf. Her father was one of the opera greats in Italy. She loved to rub shoulders with the Mob. Poor P.D., she never gave him a tumble.

I told Pussy that if she thought P.D. was a "boss," she would run after him. This set the wheels in that devil's head. Pussy called P.D. over and they cooked up a scheme to impress Roma. It went like this:

When P.D. came into the bar, and Nicky Don would announce: "We have a distinguished visitor from Florida, the great P.D." All eyes were on him (Roma's were as big as saucers), and he pretended to be very annoyed. He told Pussy, "I'm leaving. I told you I don't want anyone to recognize me."

Pussy pretended to be upset and assured him that it would never happen again. Roma asked Vinnie who the gentleman was.

"Why, the Boss of Florida," that devil told her.

Well, it worked. In fact, it worked so well that Roma wanted to marry him. This was too much for P.D., and his ardor cooled.

From that night on, any time we needed a "boss," P.D. filled the role. He was the "Boss" of Chicago, the "Boss" of Buffalo, the "Boss" of Kansas City, and so on. He played the role the role to the hilt. In fact, the local cops began to harass the poor little guy. Pat Simonetti told Dennis Walker, our favorite cop, "For Christ's sake, leave the poor guy alone. How could he be the Boss of Florida, Chicago, and Buffalo, all at the same time?" Dennis agreed, and they left P. D. alone.

P.D.'s next amour (and I think his last) was Joyce C. Bell, a pixie of a child and an exceptional dancer. She was part of a young group that hung out at the Surf, though we did not know how young until much later. She was sixteen and looked twenty. Since she never drank anything but Coke, no harm was done. Her main ambition in life was to be a go-go dancer. In the 1960s, these dancers were all the rage, and unlike today, they danced with all their clothes on.

One night, Pat decided to have a dance contest. It was a slow night, and he thought to liven up the place with his contest. Well,

Joyce won, hands down. It was a joy to watch her; P.D. enjoying more than anyone. He told her, "You are better than Eleanor Powell." This, of course, went over her head. Eleanor Powell was way before Joyce's time.

P.D. went on to tell her about the glorious Powell, and then told her that he was the one who discovered her. He said that he was a talent scout and had launched many dancing careers. This poor kid had visions of going to Hollywood. P.D. was a bit tipsy or he would never have been so cruel. I have to say that we all went along with the joke. We did not intend any viciousness; it was all in good fun. At the end of the night, P.D. promised Joyce that he would see what he could do for her.

After that night, he could not get rid of her. She haunted the bar, always asking if P.D. had been in. He began to feel sorry for her and managed to get her some bookings in various clubs that featured go-go dancing. He came to like the kid a lot and she, in turn, worshipped him.

He met her mother and frequently squired them both to fancy restaurants and Broadway plays. He became part of the family. I guess he was flattered as well that a kid young enough to be his granddaughter had a crush on him.

It all ended when Joyce invited him to escort her to her junior prom. He went on the lam, and we didn't see him for five months. What happened to Joyce C. Bell, I cannot say.

There was never anything improper between P.D. and the kid, but what I can't understand is her mother. She knew this kid was only sixteen. She had to know of her crush on P.D., and she also knew that everyone was in the dark about her daughter's age.

Maybe she was one of those horrible "stage mothers," the ones who would stop at nothing to further their child's career. Maybe she had a thing for P.D. herself. I don't know. All I know is that a cat made a better mother than Mrs. Bell.

After Pat sold the Surf in 1968, we did not seem much of P.D. I believe it was in 1973 that I heard he had died. Well, he was one of a kind. I hope God was good to him.

Chapter 16

Reetze

Of all the wonderful people in the Surf, Reetze had to be by far the most pleasant. He was shy around women and one of the few who, we believed, never cheated on his wife.

Lucille introduced me to Reetze on one of her nights off. She was having dinner with her mother, and Reetze picked up her tab. Angie, Lucille's mother, went over and kissed him, and he joined us at our table. They were talking over old times at Sardella's, the restaurant owned by Lucille's parents. They recalled how thin he was in the old days. "Yeah, in his sailor suit, he was skinnier than Frank Sinatra in "Anchors Away." Reetze was, by no means, fat. He was tall and muscular.

I asked him about his days in the Navy, and he told us a few funny stories. I told him some of my experiences in the Marine Corps. This broke the ice. We talked about Jerry Chokes (we both loved Chokes), and the night wore on.

I got up to dance with Tony Dale, who taught me to tango, and we were really enjoying the dance. Tony was a wonderful dancer; he made his partner look good.

Reetze loved to dance, too, and so we danced the night away. By the end of the night, we were fast friends. He had a wonderful sense of humor and was almost as good at adlibbing as Ray Crow.

I asked him if he knew Frank Condi. He did not. I told him that I thought they would like one another, because they had similar personalities, but Lucille did not agree. She said that both men were too handsome and would be jealous of each other. I thought the opposite, since both were handsome, there would be no jealousy. I pointed out to her that Reetze and Andy Gerard were the best of friends, and she would have to search far and wide to find two better looking guys.

I was right. When I introduced Frank to Reetze, it was love at first sight. For some reason, Reetze never pretended to be jealous of my making a fuss over Frank, but he had a great time pretending to be jealous of my love for Andy. It got to be a routine. When Reetze came in, I would tell him I loved him the most of all.

"That's not what I heard," he would say. "When Andy was here last night, you told him you love him best."

With all the look of innocence, I would reply, "No, that's not true. I feel sorry for Andy, so I tell him he is my favorite, but it's you I love."

Andy would go through the same routine, and I would assure him that I only felt sorry for Reetze, and he was the one and only.

They came in together one night, and Reetze said, "OK. Here we are. Now choose."

I told him that a lady never gets involved in sordid stuff like that.

"I guess this means we have a sit-down," Andy told Reetze.

"Oh, no, no rough stuff. I would be devastated if you did that. You two will have to fight a duel in my honor. I can't honestly choose between you."

Several weeks later, Reetze came into the restaurant and asked me to go with him to the parking lot. There was Andy with two wooden swords. The two pretended to duel in my honor. Who won? No one. I told them to stop the fight, since I belonged to P.D. It was useless to go on. We had a great laugh at that.

Reetze was the Number One Jimmy Roselli fan. He knew him personally, since Roselli was a native of New Jersey. One of my favorite Roselli songs was "Everything Reminds Me of You." One of the lines of the lyrics was "take the pictures off the wall and burn them." Reetze thought that was the song's title. As soon as he'd come into the restaurant, our bandleader Nicky Don would smile, anticipating Reetze's "Hey, Nick, sing 'Take the Pictures Off the Wall and Burn Them.'"

Reetze's first order was to "give the band a drink." This would go on half of the night, but it was the band that got drunk, never Reetze.

One night, he called Pat from Newark. When I told Pat that Reetze was on the phone, he shouted over to Vinnie, "Reetze's on the phone. Give the band a drink."

When Reetze came in the following Saturday, I told him he had a tab at the bar. He was sure he had paid his tab, and he asked if his men had perhaps left their tab for him to pay off (it would not be the first time they did that).

"No," I said. "You ordered those drinks." I went on to tell him how it came about. Of course, there was really no tab. He insisted I give him the bill anyway. "I can't let Pat get one over on me." He paid the tab.

He would tease me by saying "You belong to Pussy's mob." One night, I was mad at Pussy, and I told Reetze that some day I would leave Pussy's mob and form my own mob. This set him off on a roll. "Good idea; we'll form our own mob, with P.D. at the head. How can we go wrong?"

He suggested that we would call ourselves the "Blackfoot. We will take over Monmouth County."

I told him that my first order would be to get rid of Vinnie, because he was abusing me.

"I'll take care of him tomorrow," said Reetze. "Get his name and address." He was looking directly at Vinnie when he said that. We all had a good laugh and forgot about it.

Not Reetze. The next night, he came to the bar and threw down a black innersole. This meant Vinnie was marked for death at the hands of the "Blackfoot."

Pussy, in Florida at the time, knew nothing about it. Oh, but he would learn in time!

The night of Pussy's return to Long Branch, we were ready for him. I ignored him like the plague. I refused to wait on his table.

All he would get from me was a ghost of a smile. For a while, he ignored me, too, but by the time he was ready to leave, his curiosity got the best of him. He knew something was up. Grabbing the bull by the horns, he demanded to know "what is going on?"

I told him, "You're out. You can't order me around anymore."

He pretended to put a gun to my head. "Spill it."

I told him that while he was in Florida, we formed our own mob and that furthermore P.D. was head of the new mob.

Reetze threw a black innersole down on his table.

"What the fuck is that?" Pussy shouted.

I told him it was our logo. "We are known as the "Blackfoot Mob."

Stone silence. Picking up the innersole, he whispered, "You should call yourselves the Purple Foot, you bunch of dago bastards." And he kissed me on the mouth.

Ray Crow was confused. "Why the Purple Foot?"

I told him Pussy was referring to the old Italian method of wine making. The grapes were mashed by squashing them with your bare feet. The feet turned purple, thus the Purple Foot.

The last time I saw Reetze was in 1975. Pat had sold the Surf to Joe Agnellino. By then, I had been divorced two years and was keeping company with my present husband, Raymond.

Vinnie called me over to the bar, "Frances, look who's here." He beamed.

What a sight for sore eyes! Reetze asked about Ray Crow, and I told him Ray was in bad shape. The drinking had gotten out of hand and he had been in the hospital. Reetze wanted to know where Ray was hanging out and what he was doing for money. I told him that Vinnie and I send over a few bucks every week to help out. He sent one of his henchmen to the Commander Bar (Ray's new hang-out) with a hundred bucks.

As we were talking, Raymond came in. I introduce him to Reetze and his two bodyguards. Reetze told him what a lucky guy he was and all that other flattering nonsense of how we were Fred Astaire and Ginger Rogers at the Surf. He asked my husband if it was okay to dance with me.

When the dance was through, we returned to the bar. "Boy, what good times we had together," he told Raymond. Well, if looks could kill, Reetze would have been dead. Raymond was the jealous type. Now, if Reetze was not the gentleman he was, he could have told the two gorillas with him to throw the bum out. He realized that "the good times together" implied an affair, so he stammered "but all good, though."

I kept tabs on Reetze till 1985. Pat Merola came to live with us for a year or so, and he would see him from time to time. When Pat left (unbeknownst to us, he was dying), I lost touch. I don't know where Reetze is, but wherever he is, may God bless him and keep him always.

Chapter 17

Louie the Killer

I'll never forget the night I met Louie the Killer. I figured with a name like that he was a prize fighter. Louie had the most beautiful head of black wavy hair. He was very polite, almost shy. We were all sitting at our table. It was a very slow night. The guys were talking about some of the barroom brawls in the good old days, when Louis turned to me and said, "You know, Frances, we big guys always get the worst of it."

"I don't understand," I said.

"Well, you're sitting in a bar, and some little guy gets drunk. What does he do? He picks on the toughest guy in the place. If you don't hit him, they say, what a coward, taking that from a little guy. Everyone at the table agreed with him. "Yeah," he continued, "look what happened to me when I was in the college."

Good grief! This guy went to college! I must have had a perplexed look.

Looking directly at me, he continued his story. "Yes, we were in the yard…at the college."

I asked, "At the college?"

"Yeah, at the college. Well, there was this little guy. You know the kind that don't bother nobody, but you look at him and say *eefa*; this guy is here again. Well, the other guys were picking on him, and I felt sorry for him, so I said to them, 'Why don't you leave him alone?' Bang! Somebody hits me on the head with a brick."

I couldn't quite believe what I was hearing. In college, this happened? He was giving me a funny kind of look, as if to say, how come this teacher doesn't understand English?

"Well, did you complain to the dean?" I asked.

"Who's dat?"

At this point, I am totally confused. "Why, Louie, the dean is the head of the college."

Now, he is startled. "You mean the warden? Naw, nobody tells him nuttin'."

Came the dawn, it all fell into place. I was sitting there surrounded by the Jersey Mob!

What to do? I was a little frightened, but everybody was so nice to me. I was safer there than in my mother's kitchen. After all, they accepted me wholeheartedly.

I thought I would ask my brother-in-law, John, what to do. John was very intelligent, and he was more "street wise" than I was at the time. I'd talk it over with him.

John asked if all the customers were racketeers. No, they were not. All kinds of businessmen come to the place, even some policemen. Well, John said, "They don't involve you in anything crooked, they don't discuss their business with you, and as you said they bend over backwards to protect you."

He was right, of course. Who was I to judge anybody? There is good in the worst of people, and bad in the best of them.

A long time ago, when I was in high school, the police captain of the 42nd Precinct told me that organized crime could not exist, let alone flourish, without the aid and abetment of the crooked cop, corrupt politician, the shyster lawyer, and people's greed. I thought about that, too. At least, the gangster was no hypocrite. He was what he was, no bones about it. He stood with his bare face showing in the wind, unlike that fungus that hides behind a cloak of respectability, working hand in glove with the mobster; the mobster taking all the chances.

"My guys" had the decency to rob with a gun, unlike the insurance companies that rob with a pen, and the U.S. government solidly behind them. Why, at one time, if a person charged more than 10 percent interest, he was arrested for usury. Even back then, the banks charged 10 percent, and the credit card companies were even worse. No one put them in jail. Don't misunderstand. I don't approve of crime and all that goes with it, but who are the criminals?

To me, the three things I hated most in life were a hypocrite, a coward, and a cheapskate. My people were none of these things. Besides, I grew to love them all.

Poor Louie, he was such a gentle soul. I wondered why they ever called him Louie the Killer, so I asked Pussy.

"You don't know the story?"

"No, Anthony, I'm from New York. Remember?"

Pussy explained, "You see when Louie was seventeen, he worked for the Orkin exterminators, so his friends dubbed him Killer Lou. Besides termites, all he ever killed were chickens on his mother's farm." That name frightened the unenlightened, as the following incident shows.

One night, a young man was sitting at the bar, as drunk as a lord. Louie was berating Vinnie for serving him that much liquor.

"Louie, he came in like that. I'm giving him ginger ale, and the son-of-a-bitch is getting drunker."

Louie was always looking out for other people; he had a paternal complex. Sitting himself down next to the young man, he told him that he should have some coffee. The kid, drunk as he was, recognized Louie the Killer and asked for his bar tab.

"You don't intend to drive in that condition, do you?" the fatherly Louie asked.

The poor kid looked like he was going to pass out.

"Look," continued Louie, "you can get into an accident. Give me your keys and get in my car. I'll drive you home."

"NO! I'll take a cab," the petrified kid said.

"Look, son, don't lie to me. You want to drive home. I would never forgive myself if you left here and got into an accident. Give me the keys and tomorrow you get someone to drive you back here, and I will give you your car and the keys."

By now, the young man figured he was going for his last ride. "But I live in Point Pleasant," he said. "I couldn't let you drive all that way."

Louie told him he did not mind the long drive. By now the kid was crying.

At the end of the bar, Pussy was taking it all in. "You're scaring the kid to death," he barked. "Put him in a fuckin' cab and forget about it."

Louie did just that, paying for the cab, as well.

The next night, Pussy came in and told Louie and me to get into his car. He needed us. It seemed that Anita, Pussy's then "light o' love," was having her birthday celebration, and he had a ring specially made for her as a surprise. She and I had the same ring size, and he wanted me to try it on at the jewelers.

Off we go to Sayerville, Louie driving and Pussy and me in the back seat. The Garden State Parkway was very heavy with traffic, when Pussy spotted a dog coming out of the bushes onto the path of the speeding cars. The dog looked like it was hurt. Pussy, who loved animals more than people, was afraid the dog would get hit.

"Louie, block the traffic and see what the matter is with the dog," he ordered.

Louie was afraid of dogs. "Boss, he looks like he is hurt. He might bite me."

"And if you don't stop the car," Pussy whispered, "I might shoot you."

Louie stopped the car on a dime. He swerved to the left, blocking two lanes of the highway. It seemed like the dog knew that someone was there to help him, for he lay down in front of our car.

"Louie, get out and see what's wrong with that dog!"

I got out of the car with him. The dog was whimpering piteously, and there was a little blood on his left hind quarter.

"Boss, it looks like he was hit by a car," Louie told him.

"Put the dog in the car and get off this parkway. We'll find a vet."

Louie turned white as a sheet. This was a large golden retriever, a gentle breed, but touching a dog that is hurt could result in a bad bite. I told Louie that I would help him. We lifted the dog into the car, and he licked Louie's hand. The big lug was undone. There were tears in his eyes.

We located a vet in Sayerville. He asked Pussy how old the dog was. "I don't know. He's not my dog. We found him limping on the parkway."

The vet told Pussy that the dog's leg was broken and would require a great deal of care at a considerable cost. He reasonably wanted to know who would pay for all this.

Pussy glared at him. "Just figure how much it is and I'll pay you."

The vet looked skeptical and told him that it would come to about $200, as the dog would have to be boarded, as well as treated. Pussy gave him $250.

The vet assured him that the dog would be okay and that he would contact its owner, as the dog had a license.

Three days later, I called the vet to see how the dog was.

"Fine," they told me. "His owners claimed him this morning. They want to know the name of his benefactor so they can thank him."

Pussy was sitting next to me, and I relayed the message. His reply was, "Tell him the Good Fairy…"

End of story.

I got really close to Louie after I had been at the Surf for three or four years. You see, Vitamins was Pussy's right-hand man in the first two years we were at the Surf. When Vitamins left to go to New Orleans, Eddie Scalo took his place. Eddie was a great joker and a bit careless with Pussy's money. Pussy did not mind the joking, but the money was something else. Vinnie told me that Eddie had spent some $50,000 of Pussy's money. Since Eddie was the father of three children, Pussy would do nothing to harm him. According to Vinnie, Pussy told him "Just get out of town. If you have to pay me fifty cents a week, do so, for my prestige." That was the end of Eddie.

So, in 1963, Eddie was replaced by the ever-loyal Louie. I may have been instrumental in Pussy's choice of Louie.

"You just can't depend on these guys (Eddie and Vitamins)," Pussy told me. "They don't have their minds on business. One drank like a fish, the other was a degenerate gambler, and both were women crazy."

"Then, take Louie," I said. "Here is a guy who does not drink or gamble. He is no womanizer. He is a family man. Last but not least, he would die for you."

In Tony Dale's words, "Louie is like a big baby." Not that he was a coward; he just was not a bully. There wasn't a mean bone in Louie's body.

Pussy pointed out that Louie was not as sharp as Vitamins or Eddie. Vinnie said that maybe those two were too sharp. Anyway, I did not take too much stock in this conversation. Pussy was not one to let others make decisions for him. We all, of course, could not have cared less who became Pussy's main man. Nevertheless, everyone was delighted that he chose Louie. Because Pussy was in the restaurant almost every night, so was Louie; and a beautiful friendship was born.

Louie was a very good cook. He had owned a restaurant or two and liked the cooking end of it. I would get to the Surf at about 7 p.m., as I was in the cocktail lounge. Soon as I came in, he would greet me with "Did you eat? Do you want me to go to the kitchen and cook some scungille for you?" If I consented, he would sit down with me while I ate and tell me stories of the early days in Newark. He became my confidant.

In 1964, my husband Joe was going to Vietnam. I would be with my mother for at least fourteen months and I decided to put my son in a nearby military school. DeVitt Military Academy was in Morgan, NJ, about a twenty-minute ride from my mother's house. Louie agreed with me that it would be very good for the boy, since his father would be gone for a long time.

Two weeks before Joseph was to go to the academy, they told me that every article of clothing, every towel and washcloth had to have a label with his name sewn on. I was close to panic. The kid had twelve sets of underwear, twelve pairs of socks, twelve towels and washcloths that needed labels, in addition to his military uniforms and play clothes.

"How the hell can I get all of that ready in so little time?" I asked Louie.

"Don't worry. We will all help you. Just bring a bunch of needles and thread. The girls and I will sew with you."

Business was slow because we had received a lot of bad publicity in *LIFE* magazine. The article said that "the Surf was a gangster hang-out" and a bunch of other garbage of how dangerous it was to be there. This kept a lot of our regulars away and business slowed down to a waltz, so we had plenty of time to sew.

There were nine waitresses and Louis, all sewing away, happy as larks, when in walked Pussy.

"Louie, what the fuck are you doing?"

"Boss, poor Frances has all this sewing to do, and we're helping her."

The exasperated Pussy just shook his head and walked to the bar. Always one to take advantage to zing you, Vinnie told him,

"See, Boss, they lied in *LIFE* magazine. This is not a mob hang-out; it's a sewing circle."

During that summer, my cousin Rose Ann stayed with me every weekend. She had recently been divorced and being at the Jersey shore among my mad-capped friends helped with her depression. Her daughter Sofia was about two years old, a darling child. If it were possible to design a perfect child, Sofia would have been the result. She was very quiet and shy, always so well behaved, we could take her anywhere. She was not a big eater, a constant source of worry to Rose Ann. She never slept through the night, although she did not disturb us.

Rose Ann would come into the Surf with Sofia on a Saturday night, and we would put the baby on a pillow next to our table in the alcove, and she would sleep. If she woke up, Rose Ann was there to see to her needs.

Now this child would never go to a stranger, or so we thought. Louie was a particular favorite of Rose Ann's, and she would spend most of the night talking and laughing with him. When I was through working, I would join them, and after a while, we would all go to my house for breakfast.

The first time Rose Ann brought Sofia to the restaurant (Louie had not seen her since her marriage and divorce), he invited her to eat with them (Louie, Pussy, Anita, and so on), and put his arms out to Sofia.

"Oh, Louie, she does not go to strangers," Rose Ann apologized. Ha! She threw herself into his arms, and he kept feeding her watermelon. She fell asleep in his arms. Yes, you cannot fool young children and dogs. They instinctively know whom to trust.

That night, Sofia slept like the dead. In fact, we were up all night worrying about her. We even put a mirror under her nose to see if she was still breathing. Wonder of wonders, she slept until 9 a.m.

Around noon, Pussy and Louie brought over all kinds of cold cuts to have lunch with us. We told them how Sofia had slept, and Rose Ann mentioned that she had never seen the kid eat fruit like she had the night before with Louie.

"What fruit?" Pussy asked. "There was no fruit on the table."

We all assured him there was a whole watermelon.

"You gave that baby watermelon?" he screamed. "No wonder she slept. The watermelon was spiked with anisette."

Louie loved my children, and they loved him back. Joe, being shy did not show it; Nora worshiped him, along with hugs and kisses. He spent hours talking to her. He could not get over her extensive vocabulary. At four years of age, she told him, "You will find aspirin in the medicinal department at the supermarket." She had memorized all the presidents of the United States and could read newspapers better than he did, and he was so proud of her. He told Pussy, "This kid sounds like a Philadelphia lawyer." He won Joe's trust by giving him money to buy wooden soldiers.

Nora was six and Joe was eight when we moved from the house I had rented in Long Branch to an apartment in Keensburg. Louie found me the apartment. Though it was new with three bedrooms, it was a far cry from the lovely house on the river. On the plus side, I was allowed to have a dog in the apartment.

Nora told Louie that she wanted a Saint Bernard. Joe just wanted a dog. All Nora could talk about was getting her dog. One night, she begged Louie to hurry me into getting Diogenes. She already had the dog's name picked out. "Please, Uncle Louie, I want a Saint Bernard."

"OK, Nora, Uncle Louie will go and rob one for you."

I told Louie it would be very difficult to steal a Saint Bernard, since most of them weighed over two hundred pounds. Nora looked crest-fallen, and Louie reassured her with, "That's OK, Nora. Uncle Louie will go out and rob a puppy."

I asked him not to encourage her in this, as a dog that large would be a trial in an apartment. It would be hard for the dog, as well.

"Your mother is right. It would be a sin for a big dog like that to be in an apartment. Find a smaller dog you like, and I will get it for you."

A few weeks later, she told him she wanted a Sherman dog. He must have asked at least a hundred people, "Where can I get a Sherman dog?" While watching a Johnson & Johnson commercial, Nora had seen a lady bathing an infant. Next to the tub were a four-year-old child and a basset hound. The child says, "Please,

Mommy, can I have some of that baby powder for Sherman. He is a baby, too."

I knew nothing of this, and the great dog conspiracy between Nora and Louie. Finally, my son Joe asked me what kind of dog a Sherman dog was. Innocently, he told me the whole plot. I thought they were conspiring for a chaise lounge she wanted, which I told her she could not have, as her new bedroom was not large enough for one.

I told Louie it would be fine with me if she had a basset hound, but nothing else.

A few weeks passed, and I forgot all about it. The ever-constant Louie forgot nothing. It was my day off, and we were at my mother's house. She told Nora that someone was on the phone for her. "It's Uncle Louie, Mommy. He wants us to meet him at Walt's Furniture Store."

That goddamned Louie, I thought. He must have bought her the chaise lounge. Not so. Next door to Walt's was a pet shop. There he gave the ecstatic Nora her Sherman.

Louie took months of teasing over this, as Nora wanted him to be godfather to Sherman. Vinnie, as usual, had the last say. "I always knew you would end with the dogs, Louie."

Life in the new apartment was not a bed of roses. The family in the apartment over mine was an ignorant, useless lot. They constantly harassed my children over the dog. The kids were terrified at the father's behavior. He was always drunk and abusive.

One night, I caught him telling my children that he was going to stuff Sherman in an oven. It was my night off, and he did not know that I was at home. I confronted this big ape and told him that the next time he harassed my children he would find himself in an ashtray.

Like all bullies, he figured that since there was no man in the house (my husband was overseas), he could abuse a woman.

The mother of the family upstairs was a spiteful, sneaky woman. She knew I worked nights and needed to sleep days, so she would bang on the floor constantly. Louie saved me. If I could have grabbed her, I would have beaten the living daylights out of her and probably ended up in jail.

What happened was this: Pussy was under investigation for something or other and was in court for a week or so. Every day in the papers there were stories about him, and always on the front page. One day, as he was coming out of court walking behind Louie, the photographers were taking his picture. At that moment, Louie flipped his cigarette to the ground, and it hit the camera of one of the photographers.

The next day, the front pages of the local papers had a picture of Louie (looking terrible, like a mad dog) and the caption read: KILLER LOU SCORNS PRESS. What a farce!

Anyway, that morning, he came to my house with donuts and buns, so we could have breakfast together. As fate would have it, the witch upstairs was looking out the window as he was ringing my bell. I hear her scream, "Oh, God! Louie the Killer is downstairs. He came to bump somebody off!"

Louie asked me what it was all about. I told him about this family and that I had threatened them on several occasions. I reasoned that she had seen his picture in the paper that morning and figured I called him to bump her off. I fully expected Louie to laugh.

He was very angry. He told me I should have told him about them a long time ago. He assured me that no one would be allowed to harass me or my children.

I figured they were not worth going to jail for. He assured me that no harm would come to them, but he would "scare the shit of out them."

Two mornings later, when the husband got into his truck to go to work, there were imprints of black hands all over the truck. Did I have any trouble with them after that? No! A month later, they moved out.

After I left the Surf, I continued to see Louie. I was manager of the Arthur Treacher's Fish & Chips in Eatontown, and Pussy's office was close by. I continued to see both of them, and Louie still helped me with family problems.

Some time in the 1980s, Louie became ill with heart trouble and a bout with cancer. He survived for almost ten years.

During the time I was at Arthur Treacher's, I helped Louie in his restaurant at Belmar. Our friendship remained strong. In 1986, I left New Jersey and took up residence in New York.

The last time I saw him was on the boardwalk in Long Branch in 1987. He looked terrific. He had lost weight, he was bronzed from the sun, and his thick black hair was just flecked with gray. We spoke of the old times at the Surf and, of course, Pussy. Louie's eyes filled with tears as we recalled all the laughs we had with the "boss."

I think Louie never got over Pussy's death. We kissed goodbye, promising to keep in touch. To my sorrow, I never did. In 1989, my friend Marie Gazzolla told me that Louie had died. I was too shocked to ask how or when. I don't want to know. What can it matter?

All I could remember for a long time was the comfort I got from Louie when I lost my grandfather. I was devastated by that loss, and Louie said, "You have no guilt, Frances. You were good to him all your life. You gave him flowers when he was alive."

Louie always said, "One rose to the living is worth trainloads of roses to the dead. Give the flowers to the living."

How I regret that I did not follow that advice. I guess we are all guilty of putting off going to see a friend. Well, that's what we get and deserve in the end, around the corner, a vanished friend.

Ah, Louie, when God counts His jewels, may your name be found in pearls. I will miss you all of my life.

Chapter 18

Surf Regulars

Carlo

Carlo was Sicilian-born. He came to America when he was twelve and had a slight Italian accent. God, he was beautiful! He was in charge of the "card room" in the Harbor Island Spa. Men and women (especially women) loved Carlo. During the winter months, he lived in Florida, working at a spa in Miami. On the first of June, he would return to Long Branch, and his first stop would be the Surf.

Pussy introduced me to Carlo, saying, "Here's another broken-down *Sigi* (Sicilian). You two should get along great."

He asked the usual questions, like what part of Sicily are your parents from? Have you ever been there? And so on. He loved America, but his heart was in Sicily. This conversation was in the Sicilian dialect. As I was speaking to him, he had the strangest look on his face.

"Look, I know my Sicilian is brutal," I said. I went on to tell him that I had not spoken Sicilian since the death of my grandmother and had forgotten many words. I could still understand everything that was said to me, but I had to grope for the right words to answer. I apologized for my ineptitude in the language.

"No, *Bobedru* (Sicilian for doll), you speak the old dialect, like my mother. I want to cry; I'm so homesick."

I would sing for him all the old Sicilian songs I had learned. If he was tipsy, he would cry.

Vinnie would say, "Her singing is not so hot, but it's not that bad." He would tell Carlo, "She puts her soul into it. She is the only one who sings *encoloradi* (from the throat)." Whenever we wanted to annoy Pussy, we spoke Sicilian.

Like most of the clientele at the Surf, Carlo was generous to a fault. In spite of all the money he earned, he was usually broke. "The broads and horses are all whores," he would say. Not that he had to buy women; most of them would gladly have supported him, but he was an old-fashioned man. He paid for everything. He treated women (young and old) as if they were made of fine porcelain. Though he had many, he was always faithful to the "lady of the moment."

One night, he was at the bar completely mesmerized by this sweet young thing. He barely said hello to us, and we left him alone.

During the course of the evening, Lucille decided that we are all going to Hawaii for our next vacation.

That rude pest, John Joyce, was listening to our conversation and said, "Where would you two get the money to go there?" That arrogant bastard was always flaunting his money; he was too cheap to spend it.

Taking a look around the bar, I asked, "How much do you suppose we will need?"

With a sneer, he replied, "At least two grand."

Lucille told me to ignore him.

"OK, bastard, how much time do you give me to raise it?" I asked.

"About ten years," was the smart aleck's reply.

Now I was pissed. I told him I would raise that and more in less than half an hour and furthermore I would not have to leave the bar to do it.

Taking a paper and pencil, I started at the end of the bar. "Pat, could you lend me a hundred dollars for about ten minutes?"

He was alarmed. I never asked for money. So I told him why I wanted it. He promptly gave me three hundred dollars. So, I went down the line: Andy, Reetze, Butch, Pat Merola; all the big guns were there. They all gave me several hundred dollars. I marked it all down so I could return it, and then I came to Carlo.

"Carlo."

"What, *Bobedru*?"

"Can you lend me a hundred dollars?"

Never taking his eyes off the girl, not even turning around to look at me, he handed me his wallet. I took a few hundred dollars out and gave him back his wallet. I dumped all the money…over three thousand dollars…on John's table. With a look that could kill, he stormed out of the place.

Lucille was delighted (until I told her we had to give the money back). "What the fuck! Are you crazy? They will never miss it. Let's go to Hawaii," she said.

Lu earned more money than I did, but she was always broke. Her heart was as big as her body, so she could never hold onto a dime.

But this is Carlo's story, so on with it. Consulting my list, I returned the money to the guys. None of them wanted it back. There will never be any men like them again in my lifetime. So, I get to Carlo.

"Carlo, here is your money."

"What money?"

"The money I took out of your wallet, you dumb ass. I could have robbed you blind!"

He momentarily forgot the girl, turned to me, and said, "But you can have anything I got."

So, I told him the incident with that miserable John. He was amused, but he agreed with Lucille. He asked if I ever went on vacation. "I'm on vacation," I told him.

At the time of that incident, my husband was stationed in Parris Island, South Carolina. Knowing this, Carlo told me, "You are only an hour away from Miami by plane. Why don't you come and see me sometime?"

I told him that some day I would take a mad fit with my husband and just take off. I would get into my car and not stop till I got to Miami. He half believed me (all and sundry knew I was mad-capped) and told me he would be delighted to see me.

As the summer drew to a close, I asked for his address.

"Get in a cab and ask the driver to take you to the biggest toilet in Miami, and that's where I will be."

I was called to the phone at that moment and never took the address from him. So we parted, me for South Carolina, and he for Miami.

Just before Christmas that year, my husband decided to take the kids to Myrtle Beach for a weekend. He and I were feuding, and I was not invited. I decided to take off for Miami. Lots of the gang went there for the winter.

As I was driving down, I remembered Carlo and our last conversation. Finding him would be no problem (no, not his way, mine) so I went to the Dream Bar, a favorite hang-out of the gang, and there was Vitamins. I told him about Carlo and the biggest toilet in Miami. He gave me Carlo's address.

When I got to his apartment, he was not at home, so I told the landlady (in a Sicilian accent) that I was Carlo's sister from Italy. She let me into the apartment, and I made myself at home.

Around 2 a.m., Carlo arrived. I was sound asleep on the couch. He was thunderstruck. "*Bobedru*, how did you find me?"

"Why, I drove, like I told you I would."

"But how did you find me?"

"I just told the cab driver to take me to the biggest toilet in Miami, and here I am."

Poor Carlo, he looked so confused. Taking pity on him, I told him the truth.

"Pussy said you were smart, but he doesn't know just how smart you are."

I stayed at his apartment for the weekend, and he and his lady of the moment entertained me lavishly. Carlo later confessed that at first he was alarmed. He thought I had left my husband and was planning to live with him. You see, he loved me (like he loved his sister in Italy), but he was not prepared to marry me. His respect for me was too great. He would never have dreamed of compromising me by just living with me. My type of woman and men of his caliber married.

Carlo left the spa in the early 1970s. Larry Paskov sold the spa, and most of the employees left with him. I never saw Carlo again. Typically I never kept in touch, and when I did go to find him again, he was gone. I hope he gets to read this book and gets in touch with me. I can't think of anyone I would rather see again.

Larry Friedman

Larry Friedman was a teddy bear of a man. A brilliant metallurgist, a legitimate millionaire with a delightful sense of humor, this giant of industry was a regular at the Surf. He and his wife Rose and their son Eddie loved our food. His older son Ira was already married, and we did not see much of him.

Larry and his family were family to us. He was such an intelligent man. I would talk to him for hours on all subjects. We both loved classical music. He entertained me with stories of his boat. He loved roughing it on his boat, but Rose was a clean freak.

The boat was cleaner than the operating room at Monmouth Medical Center.

This was okay, but when she started turning it into a fashion salon, that was too much. The best was the solid brass French phone. Poor Larry, all he wanted was to have a boat; now he had a fancy bordello.

One night, I jokingly asked Larry if he would give me a job.

"What skills to you have besides being the best waitress in the world?" he asked.

"I teach history."

"Oh, well, then, I will have to marry you."

"That's fine with me, Larry, but what shall we do with Mrs. Friedman?"

A devilish grin crossed his face, and he said, "You heard of Arsenic and Old Lace?"

Vinnie, always on the Erie, quipped, "Forget about it. You two couldn't even get arrested in this town, besides Pat would go bonkers if he was short a waitress."

We pretended to consider the problem. "I have it," Larry whispered. "Mrs. Friedman will have to take your place here. I assure you she is a tireless worker. She has declared war on dirt."

I had no doubt that Rose would do a better job than I ever could do, but I could not picture the elegant Rose in P.F. Flyers. Instead of nurse's shoes that all the waitresses wore, we wore tennis sneakers. Vinnie called them P.F. Flyers, and soon everyone did. I told Larry he could forget about it, as I was sure Rose did not own a pair. He just smiled, and the night wore on.

Shortly after that night, Larry gave Rose a birthday party at the restaurant, a small affair for just family and intimate friends. The table was piled with beautiful presents. Larry handed her a box, asking her to open that one first. There, nestled between rose-colored tissue paper, was a pair of P.F. Flyers.

No one appreciated the joke more than Rose. She was such a good sport. She had a great deal of affection for me. She would pinch my cheeks and call me *Bubala*. Every time she returned from vacation, she would have a present for me.

From that night on, their son Eddie would always greet me as Mother. I'd meet him in other places, and he would run across the room, arms outstretched, shouting, "Mother!" this startled some people, as I was only about five years his senior.

Eddie was such a gay, fun-loving guy, and Larry was a little worried about him, Ira was so level-headed. Like most fathers, Larry wanted to see his son become a success. Well, my money was on Eddie, and I told him so.

One night, during the Easter season, a huckster was selling toy ducks and rabbits. They were at least four feet tall and cost only ten dollars. It was bedlam, people pushing and shoving to buy these toys. Larry was quietly eating his dinner, oblivious to it all. As I was serving him coffee, I asked, "Aren't you going to buy a rabbit?"

"No, I can't afford it," he said.

"You can't afford it! Your son just bought nine (Eddie had bought one for each waitress)."

"Oh, my son, well he can afford anything. He has a rich father."

That was my Larry.

Well, Rose is gone. May God bless her. It's too bad I did not bet on Eddie; I would have won. He started a private ambulance business in New York City, and he was a huge success. Larry, God love him, is still with us. I saw him recently in Shop Rite. He looks the same, just a bit grayer, but the same gentle smile. I was reminded that he finally did get me a job. I tell that story beginning on page 185.

Angie

Angie, Lucille's mother, came to us three years after we opened the Surf. When her father died, Angie alone ran Sardella's, a family restaurant in Newark. She wanted to be independent and refused to come and live with her daughter. Well, Newark changed rapidly from a once safe neighborhood to a death trap. Angie's health was failing (though we did not know it at the time) and after being robbed and vandalized nine or ten times, she gave up and came to us at the Surf.

This was a woman who could not remain idle, so Pat put her on as a part-time cook. I thought Lucille was the best, but she could not hold a candle to Angie.

She told us stories of the old days when Pussy and the rest were young, up-and-coming men. Mostly she talked about her

Gigi, a standard poodle that was a gift from Gyp De Carlo. She loved that dog almost as much as she loved Lucille. We bought birthday presents for Gigi, and the guys gave her money for Gigi.

Angie was the queen of malapropisms. She kept us in stitches. We never ridiculed her or laughed at her. We laughed with her.

Louie the Killer was one of her favorites, and how they indulged each other. Louie knew most of the Angie stories and with her permission he told us a few. Here is my favorite.

Sardella's was the favorite hang-out of the who's who of organized crime of the 1940s and 1950s. Our guys were then all young Turks. One night, six or seven of them ran into the kitchen and dropped their guns into Angie's apron pockets. You see, the cops were chasing them. They ran out the back door, and Angie kept stirring the marinara sauce.

"All right, lady, where did they go?" the cops demanded.

"Where did who go?" replied the unperturbed Angie.

"The guys who ran back here."

Very calmly, she said, "There is nobody here but me and my helper. You guys are seeing nightcinations (nightmares and hallucinations)."

This did not set too well with the cops. "Lady, we saw them come back here. Now where did they go?"

One cop asked her if she was smoking "funny cigarettes." He told her that if she did not cooperate, she could be prosecuted.

With that, she smacked the cop in the face. Off she went to the police station. Gyp paid the bail, and she was scheduled go to go court.

Now comes the best part.

The judge asked, "What is the charge?"

The prosecutor replied, "Withholding information and striking a police officer."

The three were in front of the judge—Angie, the cop, and the prosecutor. Withholding information was thrown out for lack of evidence. The judge asked her if she struck the officer standing next to her.

"Sure, I did. He called me a *narcotis* (a narcotic, smoking funny cigarettes) and a woman of the streets. I am a good woman."

The cop said that all he told her was that she could be prosecuted.

BANG! She hit the cop on the head with her purse, shouting, "You see, he did it again. I am a good woman."

The judge tried to explain that the cop did not call her a prostitute; he said prosecuted.

"See, even you are calling me names. What kind of judge are you? I am not *narcotis*. I am a good a good woman."

After half an hour of this Chinese fire drill, the judge had had enough. "Get this woman out of my courtroom! Case dismissed!"

From this you may come to the conclusion that Angie was dumb. She was dumb, all right, dumb as a fox. Oh, yes, the guns the guys had put in her apron pocket? How did the cops miss them? Why, she threw them into the pot of marinara sauce she was cooking. Fearing they would make a search, she created a diversion by focusing attention on herself.

We had only two years to enjoy and love Angie. In 1968, at age 55, she passed away. She had a funeral that one would expect to have been given for a duchess. I will never forget the sight of all those hardened criminals weeping unashamedly. Louie called it right when, one night, he said to her, "Angie, you're a gem." She, of course, hit him with her purse. "Don't call me names. I am a good woman." Louie explained that a gem was a precious jewel; yes, that is what she was…and definitely a good woman.

Eddie Scalo

Oh, how my people enjoyed playing tricks on one another! The divo of them all was Eddie Scalo. One early afternoon, a pretty young girl came into the place and walked over to Eddie's table. She asked him if he would help her. Would he help her? With a face like that, he would have moved a mountain for her!

It seems that she was the new inquiring reporter for the *Daily Record*, Long Branch's only newspaper. She wanted to interview him. She asked if he was a resident of Long Branch.

"Yes, dear, I am."

She asked what he did for a living.

"I'm a bookmaker," he answered.

She then asked if he would give her his name.

"Of course, my name is Pat Merola."

The next question was what could be done to improve the beaches in Long Branch.

Eddie opted for female lifeguards.

A pleasant half hour passed while Eddie put on the broad, and then she left.

Helen, in full fury, attacked the smiling Eddie. "You ignoramus! What kind of friend are you? When that article is printed, Pat the Shadow will be in trouble." With that, she threw a glass of water in his face.

Following her into the kitchen, he whined, "Oh, Helen, stop being Mother Superior. They will never print that!"

Ha! Two days later, it was printed and the Shadow went on the lam.

Rudy Lombardi

Rudy Lombardi was a musician. In his day, he was tops, playing with bands like Bunny Berrigan. In the old days, he was a trumpeter in a band at Frank Niti's (Al Capone's second in command) club in Chicago. In 1960, his days with the band were over, and he reverted to his old profession, plumbing (some may debate that).

Whatever his trade, he was always a delight. He would sit in with Sal Bertolo, a most gifted musician, who played at the Surf during our winter season. If it had been up to Pat Simonetti, Sal would have been there year-round, but for reasons of his own, Rudy preferred to work in the winter.

Like most of the gang, Rudy was a gambler, and he loved his booze. Never a problem drinker, in fact, this most pleasant man grew even more amiable when drinking.

Pat always allowed his regulars to run a tab. We had shoeboxes full of unpaid bar checks. Being a gambler himself, Pat understood when people were short of cash, and so he carried them till they were flush again and made good their markers. If a man did not pay his tab by the end of the year, Pat would carry him again the next year.

Skippy was more of a business man. You could beat him for a hundred dollars and that was it. If you did not pay at the end of the year, he would not carry you over to the next year. The only exception to Skippy's rule was Rudy Lombardi. Rudy was the exception to other bar owners, too. He was not a total dead-beat; if he had money, he would give very generously. Lots of times, he worked off his debts by doing plumbing jobs for his creditors.

Imagine my surprise when I heard that Rudy was running tabs all over town, buying drinks and dinner for all and sundry. What could have happened? I ran into him at the North Shore Inn on my day off.

"Frannie, have a drink with me, have some dinner," he exclaimed.

I asked if someone had died and left him money. He came from a moneyed family.

"No, Frannie," he laughed. "I won the lottery."

At that time, the top prize was fifty thousand dollars. I advised him to save some money. At the rate he was spending it, he would run out of cash, and some day he would need it.

"Naw, easy come, easy go," he said.

Easy come for Rudy; easy go for the unsuspecting restaurateurs. It was all a hoax. Rudy hadn't won the lottery. Did anyone have him arrested? No. Did anyone sue him? No. His brother Dicky and his nephew Kenny paid some of his debts, and some Rudy himself paid. It came as no surprise to me when some of the bar owners cancelled the debt. The latter took it all as a great joke; no one could remain mad at Rudy for long.

Livia, who should have killed him, just shrugged and said, "That's Rudy." Livia did not own a bar, but she needed a shower installed in her upstairs bathroom, as she had only a tub there. She gave the job to Rudy, and then invited me over to see the finished work.

I was looking at the shiny new showerhead and couldn't figure out what was wrong. She was laughing so hard tears were streaming down her face.

"Look at where the showerhead is and then look at where the faucet is that turns on the shower," she gasped.

Rudy had installed the showerhead on the opposite end of the tub. In order to take a shower, you had to turn on the water at one end and go to the opposite end and stand under the water.

"You are going to get someone to fix it, aren't you, Liv?"

"Are you crazy?" she said. "Why, this is the only bathroom of its kind in the world. I have a collector's item."

There was only one other collector's item of Rudy's that I can recall. Maria Gazzola owned the North Shore Inn, and one of her friends, who was opening a small luncheonette, asked her if she knew a plumber. Great-hearted Maria recommended Rudy. She knew Rudy needed money; what she didn't know was that his plumbing days were over.

Well, Rudy was hired to install a water main and a gas range. Maria was a bit nervous, as Rudy was notorious for not showing up on time, and sometimes he would not show up at all. She asked me to call Sabu, as she can't get in touch with Rudy. Sabu, another soft touch, had given Rudy work from time to time.

So, Maria finally received a call from the poor woman who was also looking for Rudy. I was having coffee with her when the call came. All I could hear on Maria's end was "What! What! Are you sure? Oh, God, hang up. I'll get Sabu there right away."

At this point, I was ready to explode. "What the hell happened? Did he show up on time for her to open her restaurant?"

Maria was staring into space. "He showed up all right. Better he should have driven his car into the ocean. Do you know what he did? He got something crossed. When the poor woman turned on the stove, water spouted out from the jets. She was too scared to turn on the water; she figured gas would pour into her sink."

Well, kiddies, that is the absolute truth. I don't know if gas came out of the water faucet, but Sabu could not stop laughing long enough to explain it all. Needless to say, this woman did not want to keep her collector's item. Sabu set it all right, and Rudy got paid for the job. What a gay Bohemian lot my friends were!

After I left the Surf, I continued to see Rudy at the North Shore Inn. For a short time, Pat Simonetti, Cheech, and I were reunited. It was fun, but the old magic was gone. We had Sal Bertolo at the organ, and Pat and I would sing and fool around on the bandstand. We had Rudy and the ever-present trumpet sitting in with us. It was Sal, a musical genius, who told me how good Rudy really was. And so it went until that fatal day.

Poor Rudy, in his early seventies, was still doing plumbing work. It was during one of the hottest summers on record that we lost him. He had a contract to repair some pipes that were in a hard-to-reach position. His helper, a nice young kid, whose name I can't remember, was late for work that day.

Rudy, as fate would have it, was early for once in his life. He should have waited for the kid, but anxious to finish the job, he crawled into the small space and got stuck under the pipes. The hot weather, his age, and I don't know what else were too much for him, and he asphyxiated. Bad enough that he died, but to die so horribly. The poor helper blamed himself; this kid has not been the same since that day.

Sal and I went to the wake together. Sal was so shaky, but under control until we saw the floral piece that Rudy's brother Dick had sent. It was shaped like a trumpet. I like to think that God needed a trumpet player for the celestial choir and so he sent for Rudy.

Joe Martinelli

As I sit here typing, little pictures flash across my mind, and here I find Joe Martinelli, who owned a large diner. He resembled Rodney Dangerfield, and he even talked like him.

I loved to banter back and forth with him, pretending to be a gold digger, and Joe, a bilked millionaire. I'd rush over to his table and in a breathless Marilyn Monroe voice, I'd say, "Oh, Mr. Martinelli, God must have sent you here today. Oh, the horror of it all!"

Grabbing my hand, and in the most inept British accent you ever heard, he would comply with, "My dear girl, how may I help you?"

Pretending to cry, I exclaimed, "Oh, the shame of it all! Oh, the sheer irony of it all! It's dear old Granny in Kansas City. You know who she always wanted to complete her college education. Well, at long last she has been accepted by Vassar. Oh, this bitter gall! Now when this dear old lady's fondest wish is about to be granted, the family finds itself temporarily short of funds."

Placing his hand over his hear, he would gasp, "Oh, no! What a calamity?"

"Yes," I would sob, "and such a niggardly sum. Mr. Martinelli, please dig and dig deep from the bottom of your bottomless pocket and give me five thousand dollars to make this dear old girl fulfill her dream."

"Five thousand, you say? Tut, tut, dear girl, 'tis a mere pittance. Consider it done."

This bit of nonsense was a boon for Helen. Whenever the guys would give her a hard luck story about needing a few dollars till they got straightened out, she would say, "You think you have troubles? Poor Frances; all she needs is five thousand dollars to send her grandmother to college."

The college bit got a bit old, so I used another tack and would greet him with "Mr. Martinelli, the worst disaster has befallen our family."

"Come, come, dear child. It can't be as bad as all that," he would respond.

"Oh, but it is. Dear old Granny in Kansas City is pregnant! Oh, the disgrace of it all!"

He couldn't help but crack a smile at that one. "But what is to be done?" he would ask.

"Well, the great German surgeon, Dr. Flippenfloppen has agreed to perform an abortion. All we need is five thousand dollars, and I know you will dig deep from your generous heart to help us."

And so it went for about four years. Whenever anyone needed money, they would ask me to go to Joe for help with "dear old Granny from Kansas City." What a sport he was! He never tired of the game. Every blessed weekend, he would be there, eagerly awaiting my next sally. Then, in 1966, it ended.

Joe had a terrible fear of flying, so when his only son was to go to college, he talked him out of going by plane. Placating him, the kid consented to driving instead.

On the way there, he was in an accident and was killed instantly. Joe was a broken man; of course, he blamed himself. We never saw him after that. I lost track of him and do not know where he is or if he is still living.

I only pray that God was kind to him in his grief. He was the best.

Richie Vonella

Richie Vonella was another willing dupe of my nonsensical carrying-on. Tall, slender, extremely good looking, and a bit shy, he never flinched when I would across the room, "Oh, that delicious Richie Vonella is here. I want to adopt him. I want to nurse and mother him."

I think I explained that I was very well endowed in the chest. Vinnie would complete the farce with, "Yes, take him to your bosom."

No one thought we were vulgar. Annie, Richie's wife, was another good sport. She would walk over to me, pretending to be angry, and say, "OK, home wrecker, I'm watching you." This started the San Alfonso nonsense.

San Alfonso was a Catholic retreat house. Christians wanting to spend a weekend or longer, just meditating in prayer, would go on retreat. It was a few blocks away from the Surf, and many of our customers went there.

Bantering back and forth on how to hide from Annie, Richie and I annoyed Lucille one night, and she turned on us like a dog. "Where can the Skinny Guinny (Richie) and Sgt. York hide from Houdini (Annie)?"

I was used to Lucille's black moods, but Richie was sensitive and hurt. Thank God I was inspired to say "Why, to San Alfonso."

The amused Lucille pulled in her horns, and a new giggle was born. Whenever a guilty assignation was desired, I would say, "Meet me tomorrow after ten o'clock mass, and we'll go on retreat to San Alfonso." The phrase caught on.

We were not being irreverent; at least, I don't think we were. Pat was a devout Catholic. He would not have tolerated disrespect to the church from anyone, and he too went along with the joke. In fact, he improved on it.

From time to time, some of the lesser gang members would get in Dutch with the law. When this happened, they would consider going on the lam for a while. Pat would tell them to go to San Alfonso instead, reasoning that not only would no one ever think of looking for them there, but also being on church property, they would consider themselves in sanctuary. This hurt no one. It relieved a lot of tension, as laughter always does. I'd be willing to bet that if the gang was around today, I would be minus this angina that plagues me.

Frankie Spoon

One of Charlie Pine's favorites was Frankie Spoon. Why he had the nickname "Spoon," I'll never know. I only know the spoon must have been golden, because that's what Frankie was, golden. Frankie had a drinking problem, but like our other people with the same problem, he was never a bother. He had a sunny disposition and a heart of gold. He always sat at Charlie's station at the bar. They were great buddies.

Frankie came into the place one summer night dressed completely in white. He looked like the owner of a yacht. Only one thing spoiled the picture; he was drunk on his ass. Seated next to him was one of our pain-in-the-neck customers, a hypochondriac that only the saintly Rita could handle.

Well, Charlie was annoyed because the lady was occupying a seat at his station that he would have preferred one of the better tippers sat in. The lady was also very cheap. So, there was Frankie, dead drunk, head on his arms, asleep at the bar. Inspired, Charlie grabbed Frankie and shook him awake, shouting, "Doctor, please get a hold of yourself. You're due for surgery tomorrow!"

The comatose Frankie just mumbled, "Let me sleep."

The poor woman was in shock. She whispered to Charlie, "That's a doctor?"

With a straight face, Charlie answered, "Why, yes, one of the finest brain surgeons in the country."

A look of uncertainty came over her face, so Charlie continued, "Yeah, we get all the doctors from Monmouth Medical Center in here. You know; a home a way from home."

With that, she ran out of the place. I wish I could say we never saw her again, but she was back the next week. One thing I can say for certain; she was very suspicious of all the doctors she saw with regularity.

Frankie laughed the whole thing off when he was told about it (he was sober by then). He told me that doctors, unlike bookmakers, could collect their debts. "You see, Frances, if the bookmaker does not get paid, where can he go? He can't go to the law. He can't go to the collection agency. So what does he do? He can only threaten the person. No, if the bookmaker does not pay a winner, he is out of business, because no one will bet with a bookmaker who will not pay off."

I guess that is why poor Frankie was not a success. He could not bring himself to hurt anyone, so they beat him out of money, since he was his own best customer (he gambled, too). I'm sure at times he could not pay off. So while he was able to dress like a millionaire, he was, in Charlie's vernacular, a broker. Still, he was worth a million laughs, and we all mourned his passing in 1984.

Joe Alphabet

Joe was Polish with a last name that used just about all of the letters of the alphabet, so that's how he got his name. He was not one of the wise guys but a regular who was known and liked by all. He was too funny, and he made cap, as you will see.

Joe was an inveterate gambler, whose wife Mary was a saint. She would not say shit, let alone curse. That is, not until this one particular day. They were scheduled to go to a christening and at the last minute, Joe told her he couldn't go; he had business to attend do.

That was the last straw. "You are going to the track with all those fuckin' bums!" Mary yelled at him.

We could not believe our ears.

"No, honey," he crooned. "You have it all wrong. We get to the track and a guy in a red hunting jacket comes out blowing a trumpet to announce the beginning of the race. Then a guy comes over the loudspeaker and says, 'Good afternoon, facing fans.' He doesn't say, 'Hello, you bunch of fuckin' bums.'"

Freddy the Horse

This story, I believe establishes Freddy as the Mercedes Benz of degenerate gamblers. He was one of the guys hanging around Pat Simonetti. At the time of this particular incident, I had not yet met Freddy. Pat told us that Freddy called him from the hospital on his death bed to place a bet on a horse.

"Come on, Pat," I said.

"Well, I go home and my wife says, 'I've been getting all these strange calls today.' The phone rings again, and I pick it up. I hear this strange voice saying, 'Matt, Matt...'

"'Yes, yes,' I say. 'This is Pat. Who is this?'"

"'Fredd...Freddy.'

"'My God, Freddy!' He was on his death bed.

"'What can I do for you?' I ask.

"All muffled and panting, I make out that he is saying, 'Go to the track.'

"'Yes, yes,' I say.

"'Put $500 on Lucky Dan.'

"'Okay, boy, take care of yourself.'

"Then I hear the nurse, 'Mr. Accera, please lie down.' There is a click and then silence."

"What happens next?" we ask.

"I put $500 on Lucky Dan."

"Oh, my God!" I say. "Did the poor man die?"

"No!" he shouts. "He should have, though. The damned horse finished last."

Freddy, too, was an inveterate gambler. I first met him at the track. I was sitting in Buddy Lepman's box, so he thought I must be somebody. He was in the next box with another track big shot, Teddy Genola. Teddy greets me, saying he was surprised to see me at the track, because he knew I didn't gamble. I told him I came only because my favorite horse was running.

Freddy naturally wanted to know the name of the horse.

"Figuda de putan," I said. [Translation: Daughter of a whore]

He said he was there for his favorite horse, too. "Cornuto." [cuckold]

Freddy and I became fast friends. Whenever we'd meet, we'd ask the other, "Is your favorite horse running today?"

Trivia

Joe Agnellino once told me (smiling affectionately) that I belonged to Pussy's Mob. Pussy said I belonged to the Parmigiano Gang, which was the most successful unsuccessful bunch of thieves you ever saw. Successful, because they were never arrested; every caper was planned own to the last detail, but unsuccessful because they never made a dime. Something always went wrong. They were way off in the clouds somewhere.

They bungled every job they ever went on. Example: they were going to steal a truck of telephone parts. It was all mapped out for them. The truck was be parked at a certain diner in a marked out spot. Well, when the time came, the spot was taken by a truck marked Marcel. They stole a truck with thousands of rolls of toilet paper! Pussy said their heads were full of cheese; hence, they were known as the Parmigiano Gang.

Well, when Joe said I was part of that gang, he was referring to my involvement with Joey "A," Ziggy, Richie Starr, and Harry Grodberg. During the slower winter months, we would pass the time playing Trivia.

In the Sun and Shore was a "Test Your I.Q." machine we loved to play. One night, the five of us scored "Idiot," so from that day on we were referred to as the Parmigiano Gang.

We were playing advanced Trivia questions: like who were the twelve apostles, name Santa's reindeer, who were the seven dwarfs, and so on. When Harry asked us to name the seven ancient wonders of the world, as we were groping for the name of the seventh, in walked a stranger. The man was dressed in good clothes with well-blended colors, but he looked like an unmade bed. He was obviously drunk, so when he answered "the lighthouse of Alexandria," we were amazed.

He asked for straight whiskey and Vinnie advised him to have it on the rocks with 7-Up. Vinnie, an old veteran, never bothered to argue with drunks. He served them plain 7-Up, and they never knew the difference. The stranger ignored us and kept on drinking his 7-Up.

At closing time, he passed out. What to do? Going through his pockets, we found a key to his room at the Sun and Shore. "Pile him in my car, Vinnie. I'll take him home," I said.

Vinnie and I managed to get him into the car. I told Vinnie the guy looked like Shipwreck Kelly, and during that summer we more often than not took him back to his motel. He never said more than three words.

All we knew was his name and that he came from Michigan. We never saw him sober. Where he went during the nights of that summer, we never knew. He always walked over to the Surf and finished the night there. He never bothered anyone; he just sat there drinking his 7-Up.

During the Christmas season of that year, the mystery was solved. The bar was jammed that night when in walked a stranger. He smiled at Vinnie and me and ordered 7-Up. We knew we had seen him before, but we could not place him. After a minute or so, the light went on. We both said "Shipwreck Kelly" at the same time. We did not recognize him. He was clean-shaven, very tidy, and very sober.

Vinnie said, "Could this be the same man? Madonna Mia, how good he looks!"

Walking over to me, he said, "Frances, may I have a table in the dining room?"

I was stunned. "You know my name?"

"Yes," was his response, "and Vinnie's, too. I want to thank you both for what you did for me this past summer."

We were amazed. We never dreamed that he knew what had been going on, so drunk was he.

He told us that he was a professor of English, a functional alcoholic, and that he spent his entire summers drunk. He went on to explain that he always spent his summers far away from home, as he feared that his alcoholism would be discovered if he were close to home.

"What made you choose Long Branch?" we asked.

He told us that he had read about Long Branch in its heyday, the days when Presidents Garfield, Grant, Wilson, and four other presidents had homes there. Long Branch was the Newport, Rhode Island of those years, and he had always wanted to see the town and, now, sober, he would.

He was aware of our kindness to him and wanted to thank us personally. He said he never found such kindness anywhere and that during the following months, "things came back to life for me."

He grasped the camaraderie among us all and said he could feel, even in his drunken haze, the love that flowed all over the place. He was inspired to go to AA and become again "a part of the human race."

You never now how the little things you do can touch, change a life. We never saw Shipwreck Kelly again. I often wonder what happened to him. If he is still alive and by luck has read this book, I want him to know that I, too, thank him. He taught me a valuable lesson. I looked at people differently after that incident. How ready we are to toss away a person if they do not measure up to our ideals. We see a drunk, a prostitute or any other dreg of society, and we write them off as unworthy. He taught me the "sin of pride," and I became a better person because he touched my life. God bless you, Shipwreck.

Chapter 19

The Girls

I have passed over the other waitresses—Rita, Patty, Joan, Elsie, Rosemarie, and Ronnie—because they were not a part of the group. They had different personalities, far less mad-capped than I. Helen was far from mad-capped, but I was closest to her, and she was so gutsy and so talented that she stood out.

Rita was a lady to her fingertips. She was quiet and a bit shy. If Pat Simonetti was the heart of the Surf, Rita was its soul. She set it all up. Planning with Pat the menu and décor, she set up the system of how to order the food and how to time the order so the appetizer did not come out at the same time as the main course.

My first three years were spent in the cocktail lounge. Rita was head waitress in the dining room. People tend to be more relaxed when drinking than when dining, and I therefore had a different rapport with the customers.

Rita was loved and respected by all, but she had her man (mine was always in the jungle somewhere), her kids were grown, and she spent time with them. I had more time to spend with the guys. I went bouncing a few times with Rita (when she was mad at

Alex), and she was a delight. She taught me a lot about formal dining, and her dignity awed me.

When she remarried in 1964, she left the Surf. We were reunited briefly when Joe bought the place. She worked part-time then; Helen had left by then, and I was now head waitress. Rita would affectionately call me "Boss Lady." We had a lot of ties that bound us together, but we lost touch when her health forced her to retire. I blame myself for not keeping in touch and would give the world to see her again.

Patti was a bit shy, also. Unlike Rita, she had a pixie kind of humor, always playing practical jokes and being a good sport when the joke was on her. I think it was when Patti left (for a short time) to go to Florida to live that I took her place in the dining room.

Patti and I were reunited when Joe bought the place. During Pat's ownership, she usually went home after work. Her children were younger than mine, and she did not have the advantage I had. My kids were safe at home with my mother and since I had no husband waiting at home for me, I could go bouncing after closing time.

I am fortunate that since Patti and I still live in Long Branch, I get to see her now and then. Helen used to say we would all end up in an old ladies' home and play cards together.

Rosemary (Roe) was a very pretty natural redhead. Quiet and shy, she was the mother of four boys and she, too, went home at night. Roe was always sunny, and she used to hum a lot. She enjoyed the band and was a great favorite of Reetze. She was always talking about her boys. I loved listening to her; she had this delightful, breathless, little girl voice.

Ronnie was a student at Monmouth College. She was the Gunga Din of the Surf. She was our cashier in the summer, the cloak room attendant in the winter, the shopper for fresh vegetables, and sometimes a fill-in waitress. A tall, blond, tireless worker, she was devoted to Helen, a friend to all.

I encouraged her to go out and see the world. In 1969, we were going to go to Russia together, but I bought my house that year and could not afford to go on the trip. I loaned Ronnie my mink coat (Pussy's birthday gift), and you would have thought I had given her the Hope diamond.

She confessed that it almost ruined the trip. She was so worried that she might lose it. She didn't; I still have it.

Anyway, she went on a trip some years later to the Arab World. She loved it so much that she got a job in Kuwait and lived there for many years.

On a trip to France, she brought back a painting for me because she said it reminded her of Russia. I still have the painting but I would trade it gladly to have Ronnie again. I miss all of our talks over the years. I was very remiss with Ronnie. I should have written to her while she was in Kuwait. I should have kept in touch with her, but I did not, and so I deserved to lose her.

Forgive me, Ronnie. I always valued you, but like most people, we reserve all of our courtesies for strangers; those near and dear, we neglect.

Joan Murphy was with me in the cocktail lounge. Her husband Bob was devoted to her and picked her up at work each night. She and Elsie were very close and saw a great deal of each other. She came to breakfast a few times with us, as she adored Pat Merola, who always picked up the tab, and he returned the feeling. She would tease him unmercifully, but he more than held his own. Ah, they were a delight!

At that time, I was renting Nutsy Fagin's home, a riverfront property, and she came by boat to see me. One day, I was out when she came. She took my Nora and Pat's boy Tommy for a boat ride. When I returned, Joseph told me "A man came here, asked for a book of matches, and took Nora on the boat."

Well, I panicked. I thought Nora had been kidnapped. My next door neighbor was Sgt. Gibson of the Long Branch Police Department. I ran to his house and told him Joe's story. He called the Marine Police, and they located the boat.

Joan was mad, but when I related what my nine-year-old son had told me, she got even angrier. "A man? He said a man? For God's sake! I had my hair in curlers. Do I look like a man?"

Poor Joe thought she was an Arab and that the scarf on her head was a turban. With her terrific tan, well, to him she looked Arabic.

With that, we burst out laughing. Joan was very blond, and blue-eyed, to boot. She took a good ribbing over that incident. Pat asked her why, if she was going to kidnap anybody, she picked Nora. Everyone knew that "Frannie could not hold onto any cash."

Joan went out of my life when Pat sold the place. I do not know where she is now. I heard that her husband died, but no one knew where Joan was at the time. I think she moved to Clearwater, Florida.

I am sure that if we all collaborated on this book, it would have been five thousand pages long; after, we all had our little Surf stories to tell. Maybe some day…

Helen

When Pat closed the Surf, Helen and I had to find another job. In the Channel Club, a private club where most of the members owned yachts, Larry Friedman had the biggest yacht. Walter M., owner of the club, was a customer of ours, so we felt sure of getting a job there.

We went for an interview with Walter's club manager, a snob from the word go. He of course asked us where we had worked before, and we told him the Surf. He proceeded to inform us that he was sure we would not fit in at the Channel Club, as it had a very different clientele.

This was too much for fiery Helen. "I don't think so. We have a lot of Channel Club members as steady customers," she said, dripping with venom.

Arching his eyebrows, clearly indicating that he suspected she was lying, he mimicked, "Like who?"

By sheer chance, she hit on the right one. "Like Larry Friedman," she said in a dulcet tone.

Now, this fop was annoyed. "It just happens that I know Mr. Friedman very well," he said.

"Well, smart ass, why don't you call him?" Helen snapped.

He did just that. "Mr. Friedman, there are two women in my office applying for a job, Helen and Frances from the Surf," he said in a voice of clear disdain.

Larry was so excited; he shouted into the phone, "Helen and Frances are coming here? Oh, you lucky man!"

Well, we got the job, and the manager's undying hatred.

Ah, Helen, will I ever see the likes of you again?

Walter was delighted to see us, and Helen lost no time telling him what she thought of his manager. Did he fire us? Hell, no! He was such an amiable giant and not only in height. Many a night, he cooked or washed dishes, if the necessity arose. He was so good-natured; no pretense about him. He knew his manager.

There was Helen with all her feathers unruffled saying, "Imagine, Walter, he had the nerve to ask if there was anyone who would recommend us!"

Smiling ever so gently, he asked, "Why didn't you tell him, yes, Monmouth County?"

Walter took a fiendish delight in the "battle of wills" between Helen and the rest of his staff. The crew of the Channel Club was a great bunch. Peter, the maitre d', like the manager, was a snob. He was also greedy. Unbeknownst to Walter (who would have fired him on the spot if he knew), you had to kick back to him from your tips, if you wanted better tables or better tippers.

Helen and I preferred to remain in "Siberia" than go along with that. We were not cheap; we gave freely to the captains and busboys that helped us. This haughty bastard earned three times what we did. Why should we be hustled? Principle was involved. The others thought Helen was stubborn. (I probably would have gone along with it, but I was too lazy to bother.) Anyway, they would call it stubborn, and Helen and I called it integrity.

After a month or two, the maitre d' got his comeuppance. He, too, had to swallow it, because most of the favored customers were our old customers, and they were delighted to see us. They embraced us, laughed with us as equals, and this annoyed Peter. He got even, though, in small petty ways, making sure that none of them ever got to sit at our station. Never, that is, until the night Frank Gabriel came in.

I was alone on that particular night. Helen had gone home early as she did not feel well. It was not too busy, because it was the winter season. The waitresses were kept busy. My station was half empty, as usual, when I spotted Frank at the bar.

"Hello, Frank. How nice to see you."

"Frannie, my God, I didn't know you were here."

We spent a few moments talking, and he asked if I would take care of his table.

"Frank, here we have protocol. You have to ask the maitre d' for my table," I explained.

Frank was a diamond in the rough, having come from humble beginnings and rising to the rank of millionaire. He owned several nursing homes throughout the state. He dressed beautifully and lived an elegant life, but he never put on airs. He looked like a dandy, but he was no cream puff.

It was going to be interesting to see how our maitre d' handled this one. An hour went by, and Frank was still waiting at the bar for a table. Calling me over, he asked, "Are you busy?"

In tones of milk and honey, I replied, "Why, I am not busy at all, Frank."

"What do you mean?" he asked. "The host told me your station was busy, so I said I would wait."

With a smile, I told him, "I hope you are prepared to wait all night till we close, because you will never get my table." I then told him the situation.

"Is that so? We'll see about that."

Gone was Mr. Nice Guy. It was a different Frank who asked Peter if my station had a table for him now. Of course, Peter told him the same bullshit, that my station was full.

Rising to his full six feet, four inches, Frank grabbed Peter by the lapels and hissed in his face, "You bald-headed bastard, I am going to have Frances for my waitress tonight or I'll turn this friggin' place into a warehouse."

He got my table, and Peter got off my back.

Six months after that incident, Helen and I went back to the Surf. Joey Agnellino had bought it and asked us to come back. I felt like a heel leaving Walter, but I was going home.

Helen? In 1980, after a gallant three-year fight with cancer, she succumbed to the disease. What courage she had. She knew she was dying, but she faced it all with humor and dignity. For a full six months, we practically lived on her king-sized bed. We never knew how we would find her.

One day, she was Truman Capote, complete with large glasses on her head and a slouch hat, sounding (and looking) exactly like him. On Valentine's Day, we'd find her with red paper hearts stuck all over her bald head. She never complained about the pain, and she never pitied herself. She fought with all she had. She taught us a lesson in how to bow out gracefully. She was a joy.

The last time I saw Helen was on December 17, 1980. I was leaving for England the next day to visit my daughter for Christmas. We sat on the bed, and she asked her daughter Susan to bring in the "broken cookies we baked for Christmas." She apologized for not giving me the whole cookies, as she was saving them for her guests on Christmas Day.

We laughed over old times, and she kept urging me to try this cookie or that candy.

"God, Helen, take these things away. They are like drug addiction. I can't stop eating them."

"You're right," she said. "I'm not supposed to eat them. I am diabetic. They are no good for me."

She would never admit to anyone that she was dying.

"Helen, you think we might get sick and die if we eat any more?" You could say things like that to Helen.

Now, it was time to take my leave. Promising to write, I prepared to go. She gave me large pink booties that she had crocheted for me. "It's cold in England; you'll need these."

Smiling, I said goodbye.

"Well, aren't you going to kiss me goodbye?"

"But, Helen, you never want to kiss me. You're forever saying I have a cold."

"Well, never mind that now," she said. "Kiss me goodbye. You will not see me again."

That stopped me cold. "Helen, I'm going away for only three weeks. I'll be home on the second of January."

"That may be," Helen said in the old schoolteacher tone, "but I will be gone by the time you get home."

I started to cry. "Oh, Helen, you've hung on so long. Can't you hold on for three more weeks?"

With such a sweet smile, laced with a bit of sadness, she answered, "It's not up to me, Mother (our nickname for each other). I just know these things. On the day you arrive, they will have already buried me."

Helen was a bit clairvoyant, so I came home two days earlier, as I feared she would prove right. She did. When Raymond met me at the airport, the first thing I asked was, "How is Helen?"

He shook his head. "We buried her this morning."

I could go on and on about my irreplaceable friend, but this is not Helen's story. Her last request was to be cremated and for us to scatter her ashes over the Surf. She told her children that her happiest years were spent there and that was where she wished to remain. It was, of course, against the law to do that, but we did it anyway.

I've been told by doctors that patients who died and were brought back to life shared a similar experience. Most of them said that a loved one would come to greet them. I hope that it's true and that when it's my time to go, Helen comes to greet me. I can hear her now, "Well, Mother, you took your sweet time getting here."

Chapter 20

Anthony "Little Pussy" Russo

Now we come to the main event: Pussy. I have saved the best for last. He was in the Surf most every night, and I couldn't wait to see him. In he would come with his entourage, his men, his toadies, his friends; he seldom came alone. Always dapper, very seldom in a bad mood, and a real kibitzer; he loved to make me angry. He wanted to see the reaction of his followers when I would tell him "go kill yourself."

One night, Pussy walked into a deserted restaurant. He was out of sorts (it showed on his face). "What room is the wake in?" he asked.

Well, when he was in a bad mood, everybody was nervous; everybody but me. I said, "Boss, we are sitting on a million dollars."

He gave me that fish-eyed look. "Yeah, who robbed a bank?"

"Well, some guy wrote a book called *The Gang That Couldn't Shoot Straight*, and now Hollywood bought the book."

"Oh, yeah," Pussy said. "That guy had a lot of inside information. They did have a lion in the basement to help collect outstanding debts. That crazy Joe Gallo brought in the lion."

"Well, there you are," I said. "We could write a book."

"Forget about it," he growled. "The FBI knows how to read, too."

"No," I said, "we will write about all the funny things that happened. We have people here that are funnier and certainly more stupid."

Now he was grinning. "Oh, you mean the Parmigiano Gang?"

"Yes, and we have a lot of inside information here."

He was getting impatient. "OK, you *Sigi* bastard, get to the point."

With a triumphant note to my voice, I announced, "Let's write a book. Hollywood buys the book, and we are made."

Well, everyone fell in with the joke that we should write a book.

From Pussy: "You'll have to change the location of the place."

From Patty: "Instead of Long Branch, we could call it Short Twig."

From Louie: "Christ, you have to change the names."

Now, all were volunteering suggestions. "Look, Boss," I continued, "I'll change all the names."

"Tell me," Pussy whispered, "what are you going to call me?"

"Why, Kitty Kat, of course."

This brought a chuckle. "And what are you going to call Louie the Killer?" (This he said with a sneer.)

"Oh, Large Louie the Enforcer."

"You know, Frances, you are fuckin' nuts, but it is crazy enough to work. You have to think of a good title, though, because the title sells the book."

"Oh, I have thought of a good title. I'll call my book *Cops and Wops.*"

"You can't call it that, you *Sigi* bastard!"

"Why not?" I asked.

"The Italian Civil Liberties Union won't go for that shit."

And so the phantom book was born. This farce went on for years. Every so often, I would call him to tell him the latest developments. It was a good ruse when he was sad or out of sorts.

We had a small TV set in the kitchen, and on slow nights, we would watch all the old movies, especially the old gangster flicks from the 1930s and 40s. Pussy used to imitate James Cagney or George Raft, who were imitating gangsters.

I asked Pussy why he didn't wear a black shirt and white tie like all gangsters wore. He told me a very interesting thing. He said that the mobsters adopted that look from George Raft; no gangsters before his time dressed like that.

I did not believe him; then years later, Raft wrote a book and said he was the one who invented the "gangster look" and that the real gangsters had copied him.

For a long time, I could never tell when Pussy was putting me on. He told the most outrageous lies with a straight face. If I was on the phone with him, I could not tell at all. He got me in hot water sometimes with his little jokes.

In 1964, my husband was stationed in Kansas City. In those days, I worked the summer months, so come winter, I would call the Surf once a week to see how everyone was doing.

One night, I called and Lucille put Pussy on the phone. "Hello, honey, where are you now?"

"Kansas City."

"You are so close to Vito (Mr. Genovese was in Leavenworth Prison that year). Why don't you go and see him?"

"How can I do that? I'm not on his visiting list."

"Just call them up, tell them you're a friend of the family, that you heard he was sick, and that you would like to see him. This way, when you come home for Christmas, you can tell Nancy (Vito's daughter) that you saw him."

Dumb me, I did just that. I called the prison and asked about the procedure for visiting a prisoner when not on the inmate's visiting list."

"What is the prisoner's number?" the receptionist asked.

"I don't know."

"Well, what is the prisoner's name?"

"Genovese. Vito Genovese."

Stone silence on the other end. "Just one moment, please."

I heard a click and then someone picked up the phone. "Warden speaking."

Dear God, I got the warden! "Look, I don't want to bother anybody. I just want to know how to visit a prisoner. I am not on his visiting list."

"You will have to write to the parole board for permission," the warden said.

I did just that. I told the parole board the story that Pussy told me to say. A week later, I got an answer: "Due to unfavorable publicity, Mr. Genovese does not wish to see anyone."

I was disappointed, but a few days later I got a call from Leavenworth. Mr. Genovese had changed his mind. If I would be at the prison the following Tuesday, he would see me. When I got to the prison, I was ushered into a private room, not the visitors' hall. It was just a small room with a desk and two chairs.

In comes Mr. Genovese. He is thunderstruck at seeing me. "Figlia mia [Translation: my daughter], how did you get here?"

I told him the story.

Shaking his head, he said, "That Pussy. Don't you know he was joking?"

He knew nothing about my call. It was all bullshit. They wanted my address to see who I was. He feared that I would be on the FBI's list in Washington.

"I am already there," I told him. "I was in the Marines."

"No, no, no," he said, "they will have you down for Mafia affiliations and would be sure to tap your phone."

I forgot all about it. When I got back to New Jersey, I received a telegram from my husband, which read, "Help! The FBI is after me!"

I showed the telegram to Pat Simonetti. "What ever possessed you to try and see Vito?" he asked.

So I told him.

"Didn't you know that Pussy was putting you on?"

"How the hell could I know that? I couldn't see his face. My husband calls me to say that the FBI came into his office and wanted to know what my 'connection was with Mr. Genovese.' He assured them that I was not a gun moll or anything like that; just the true story. I worked for his son-in-law, was a friend of Vito's daughter, and thought she would appreciate a person from home visiting her father."

That was not the end of the story. The FBI investigated my husband all the way back from the time he was eighteen years old. He was to go overseas, and his departure was delayed a few months. Last but not least, I was placed on the FBI's list as a "Mafia connection."

We later learned that Mr. Genovese never said he did not want to see me. He told Pat, "The only person I see is the priest. I can't even have the Italian newspapers."

I don't know if I'm still on the FBI's list; if not, this book should earn me a separate list all my own. Bah, what nonsense!

From time to time, I would get angry with something or other at the restaurant, and I would tell Pussy, "I quit! Shove this job up your keester for Easter." He, in turn, would ignore me.

One night, I was really mad and he knew it, because I was whispering, and I called him Pussy. "Anthony, this time, I mean it. I quit!"

Looking at me in mock horror, he whispered, "Chief, you can't quit the Mob. Look what they did to John Garfield in that picture when he wanted to quit the Mob."

Of course, my good humor was restored, and the night went on.

With all his sterling qualities, his most outstanding one was that he was able to take a joke on himself. We never feared him or what he would do if we angered him, and so we gave as good as we got.

Louie Coca Cola was a long-time friend that Pussy loved to tease. Poor Louie had ulcers and had to eat certain foods. After each meal, he would ask, "You got a little fruit, Frances?"

One night, we had a watermelon cut out like a basket and it was filled with all kinds of fruit. It was left-over from a small banquet that afternoon.

Pussy had to leave early that night, as he had a flight to catch early the next morning. As he was leaving, he told me, "When Louie Coke asks for a little fruit, bring him the watermelon and tell him it's on me."

When Jo-Jo and I carried the watermelon to Louie's table, he said, "I would like to send it to Pussy's house for a *bon voyage* gift."

Anita coos, "Oh, please, Louie, he will love it."

So, I got dressed in a busboy's uniform, and Louie called a cab for me to deliver it.

"Take me to 89 Jerome Avenue in Deal," I informed the cabbie. Well, we were looking for the number and couldn't see it. Some houses did not have addresses, and the numbers we could see were all crazy. They did not follow in sequence. One house was 119, the next was 123. What happened to 120, 121, and 122? The cab driver told me there was no such number as 89. I insisted there was.

It was now 11 p.m. "Look here, cabbie, Mr. Russo has lived at that address for eight years. There is such a number!"

With that, he stopped the cab on a dime. "Miss, you are going to Mr. Russo's house at this hour?" (Pussy was known to go to bed early, because he was an early riser.)

"Of course," I told him.

"Look, miss. I'll take you to his house, but I will not get out of the cab to help you carry that watermelon."

So, we finally arrived at the house. I rang the bell (musical chimes) and after a few moments, Pussy opened the door. There he was in this bright orange terrycloth robe with wisps of auburn hair in disarray.

"Ah, *Fongool*, you and Louie Coca Cola and that watermelon…"

I told him Louie thought he would like a piece of fruit.

"Take that watermelon, cut it in half, and shove one half up your ass and the other half up Louie's."

The cab driver was sinking in his cab. We woke up Pussy.

Now, he was smiling. "Frances, take that back. I can't take it with me to Florida. It will spoil here. Do you want a cup of tea?"

I declined and told him good night.

"Good night, you *Sigi* bastard. I love you."

Hearing that, the cabbie perked up again.

When I returned to the Surf with the watermelon, Anita tearfully asked, "Didn't he like the watermelon?"

"I don't know if he did or not, Anita, but Louie and I have a sex problem." This, of course, went over her head. Louie, the super hep guy, figured it out.

When Pussy got back from Florida, he enjoyed telling the story, explaining to Vinnie "They were smart to send her. If it was anybody else that woke me up, I would have shot him in the leg."

My second husband Raymond was called Sir Raymond. His dress and speech was always impeccable. Raymond adored Pussy, but always called him Mr. Russo. This was out of respect, not fear. Pussy, in turn, liked Raymond. This was known to all, as he never failed to invite Raymond to "sit down and have a drink." The few people Pussy did not like were never invited to sit at his table. He loved teasing Raymond, who was so gullible. Here is Raymond's favorite Pussy story:

Raymond came in at 10 p.m. one night and, as usual, he was invited to have a drink. *"Francesa, veni qua.* [Translation: Frances, come here.] Get your husband a drink."

As I handed Ray the drink, Pussy continued, "Raymond, how come you married this broken down *Sigi?*"

Raymond hesitated for a moment. "Because I love her, Mr. Russo."

"YOU LOVE HER! Don't you know she buried four guys already?"

Poor Raymond, he did not know how to take that remark. Pussy was still new to him. So I gave Pussy my classic reaction to his juicing me, "Go kill yourself, Anthony." This put Raymond at ease, with Pussy laughing hardest of all.

Sometimes just the thought of Pussy getting upset could change a situation. I had an old air conditioner at home that worked but made noises like a plane taking off. I told Raymond and my son to put it in the street for the garbage collectors.

Six months later, they put it on the porch. When I came back from work, the air conditioner was gone.

At work the next night, I told the girls about this strange happening. Ace, our black dishwasher, came to the table. "Miss Frances, did you get your air conditioner?"

"Hey, Ace," I hollered, "what do you know about the friggin' air conditioner?"

"Well," he says, "I heard them talking at the Tally-Ho bar (a neighborhood bar in the black section of town) about the nifty air conditioner they ripped off from that big yellow house on Rosewood. I said to them, 'Do you know who lives in that house? Miss Frances from the Surf.'"

With that, they put the air conditioner back on my porch. They were afraid that Pussy might break their heads.

Most people were under the impression that Pussy could not read or write. This was not true. He went as far as the fifth grade, and his handwriting was childish, but he could read very well, as the following incident proves.

Friends from New York came to visit me on my day off. We bought some plastic pith helmets and after one day at the beach, we went into the Surf. We looked like we were dressed for safari. Vinnie hollered over to Pussy, "Look what the wind blew in."

Going over to his table, I asked, "Dr. Livingstone, I presume?"

In a very good Cockney accent, he replied, "Quite, quite, my dear Stanley."

Well, it turns out that as a boy he had read the story of Stanley and Livingstone. He read all the newspapers, and his comments were hilarious.

He was reading the paper that night and after greeting me, he said, "Boy, oh, boy. Look at this. It says here that King Farouk wishes to build a university in the United States, and the government turned him down." This he said with a straight face.

So, I bit. "What for? For Christ's sake, we can't have too many schools."

"Well," he continued, "he had only one request, that the university be named for him."

"They turned him down for that?" I screamed.

"Yeah, they did not want a university named Farouk U."

What a quick wit that man had, and I have proof positive that he could write, as I have a little note from him.

There were quite a few celebrities in the place one night—Walter Reed, Marty Allen, Jackie Leonard, Phil Valipiano, the football star, and a few more.

Well, Pussy had made the front page of the local papers that day, something about unions. All nonsense, but they dragged out everything from his past. It did not impress us at all. We were used to all the garbage that was printed about him.

I spent my usual time at his table, taking his dinner order, and for some reason or another, everything that came from the kitchen was wrong.

"Jesus Christ!" he bellowed. "What's happening? I know there are all kinds of big shots here tonight, but what am I, chopped liver?"

Damn, just when he was going to do something nice for Chang, our busboy, this happened.

Chang and his brother escaped from China and were sending their money to their family. This Chang was so good. Instead of going to Chinatown on his nights off (like the other Chinese kids at Jimmy-Loo's), he saved all his money to send to Mama. He never spent a dime on himself.

Helen bought him clothes, explaining that he had to be properly dressed for a busboy. Half he sent to China. Pussy knew this and thought it admirable.

Poor Chang, he did not understand that Pussy's hollering was no threat. Pussy's whispering was another thing. So the kid was afraid to go near his table.

I waited about an hour, and then I went to his table and asked if I could have his autograph. Taking my order pad, he signs, "I love you, Pussy." He got the message, as far as I was concerned. He was the only celebrity in the place. When he told me I was fired, I knew all was well, so I told Chang to take him his black coffee.

"You, Chang, come over here." The poor kid was trembling. "Give me your right hand," he said pointing to Chang's right hand. The kid was so rattled. "This fifty dollars is for Mommy. Now give me your other hand. This fifty dollars is for you to spend on yourself. Do you understand?"

Chang just stared at him.

"Kid, if I find out that you did not spend money on yourself, I am never going to give you money again." He went on to tell him that his mother would want him to have some money for him and that she would understand and want him to enjoy a little bit in life, too.

Now, Chang was smiling, thanking Pussy. He told him he would spend the money on himself. Of course, he sent it all to his mother. Did Pussy never give him a dime again? No, he gave him double. This man was good to his mother, too.

Jo-Jo was another favorite of Pussy's. She too had no fear of him and answered back in his own kind. She was quicker witted than I, and he loved her for it. The story that was the funniest Jo-Jo encounter went as follows:

Pussy was having out-of-town guests, and he picked the busiest night of the year for this. We were told to put on the dog; these were important people.

We were all running around like crazy. As luck would have it, he was in a very playful mood. "Is my wine chilling?"

"Yes, Mr. Russo."

"Did you get my artichokes?"

He had already seen the damned artichokes cooking. And so it went for an hour, stopping me every five minutes with inquiries about the wine. He did not realize that he was making it harder for us. I had no time to fool with him, and the others were suffering, too. They had to pull their own weight and half of mine. He was trying to get a rise out of me. This time, I thought, he will not get to me.

Well, after an hour of this nonsense, I was beginning to crack. I brought the wine and went through the unnecessary motions, pouring a little wine into his glass for him to taste first. This was horseshit; he just drank the wine.

As I was walking away, he grabbed my arm, "Wait, I want to smell the cork."

Enough was too much. "YOU WANT TO SMELL THE CORK? This goddamned wine is $3.50 a *case*, and you want to smell the cork?"

Jo-Jo was taking it all in. "I got his cork," she shouted. "Right here, between Broad and Market. Tell him to smell this."

That devil Pussy was studying the faces of the important guests. They looked as if they had been hit by lightning.

Now, I thought, I will end this farce. "Go kill yourself, Anthony. I'm busy."

You would think that by now his friends would have been used to him, but they were not. He was chuckling; they were shaking their heads in amazement. I don't know what he told them, but it must have been good, because every one of them tipped me as they left. Vinnie reasoned that he told them I was crazy, and they felt sorry for me. If that was the case, what did he tell them about Jo-Jo? They did not tip her.

Raymond and I were going to Italy. We went to the Surf to say so long. In came Pussy. "We're going, Boss. Do you know anybody in Sicily? I promised my grandmother on her death bed that if I ever got to Sicily I would visit her mother and father's graves."

Nodding, he said, "Yeah, I know Miguel oo Zorpa. [Mike the Gimp.]

"Oh," I said, "who is he when he is not at home?"

Shaking his head, Pussy replied, "the Boss of Sicily."

"Great, I go all over Sicily and ask any stranger for Miguel oo Zorpa. That should go over like a lead fart. Sicilians are suspicious of everybody, mostly Americans."

Pussy gave me a fish-eyed look and continues. "No, smart ass, I'll dial Sicily 1234 and tell them you are coming."

We all laughed at that and kissed one and all good-bye.

We went to Italy, a package tour of fifteen days that did not include Sicily. So, we forewent three days in Assisi and flew from Rome to Sicily. I don't know why, but we had to go through customs from Rome to Sicily, I got out of the long line to take a picture of the plane. On all of our trips, I took pictures of everything for Bubby, Raymond's nephew in Las Vegas. He had been in a wheelchair from the time he was two, so this way he lived vicariously on our trips.

As I got ready to take the picture, a police officer shouted at me, "No flash!"

Two strange-looking men came over and pointed at me, telling the officer something in Italian. The official came back. "Senor McKee? Take your picture."

I looked at Raymond, and the two men approached. "Signora McKee, don Miguel is waiting for you."

That damned Pussy really had called Sicily!

From this beautiful old Mercedes, a man about Pussy's age welcomed me to Sicily. For once in my life, I was tongue-tied. I remembered to kiss his hand for respect, and I told him (in Sicilian, of course), "The cat sends his regards."

Laughingly, he said (in perfect English), "That damned Pussy never changes."

I was amazed that he spoke English so well. "Oh, we came to America when I was thirteen. Eight years ago, they deported me."

He had come to take us to lunch and to ask if there was anything he could do for us. He had already found my grandmother's family, her sister-in-law, and her nephew. He gave me a card with his telephone number and the number of a private cab company.

The next day we arranged with the cab driver, Vincenzo Pantano (most Sicilian men are named Vincenzo, Sophio or Salvatore) to pick us up and take us to the little town of Sortino. I was truly excited. All the way up the small mountain, I kept telling Vincenzo to stop the cab so I could ask all the passers-by we met if they could tell me where the family of Rosa Di Lorenzo lived.

Vincenzo told me I was going about it all wrong. We got to the piazza, and this crowd surrounded the cab. He asked them to send him the oldest living person in the village.

"Bruno," they shouted. Cap in hand, this little old man approached the cab.

Vincenzo told him that I speak Sicilian and asked if he knew the family of Rosa Di Lorenzo.

Nodding his head, he said, "Santino [my grandmother's nephew]."

Now it was Vincenzo's turn to be amazed. "These people really live here," he said and asked Bruno to direct us to the house. We learned later why he had not mentioned that my Aunt Santina was alive. She had thrown him out a year ago and as far as he was concerned, she was dead.

When we arrived there, Bruno refused to enter the house. Inside, I saw a small room divided in half by a curtain and a bed with an old lady in it. She looked like my Aunt Sandy.

"Who are you?" she screamed.

I told her that I was the granddaughter of Rosa Di Lorenzo.

"My child," she shouted. "Go behind the curtain."

There I saw a stove, a small refrigerator, and a small table. On the walls were pictures of my entire family.

By now the whole town was outside the door to see what was going on. I told her all the family news, who had died, who had gotten married.

She told me that my grandfather's niece, who lived behind her, had thrown her down a flight of stairs because she wanted her house. The house had been a wedding present to my grandmother from her father. When she came to America, she left the house to her brother and, so now, according to law, the house was hers and had nothing to do with the Cartelli branch of the family (my grandfather's side).

Sighing, she said, "American law. We are in Italy."

I told her not to worry; I would contact my family and straighten it all out.

"Oh, how good you are, just like your grandmother."

My grandmother had sent her money for years, and then when World War II started, all correspondence to Italy ended.

I gave her the jewelry I was wearing. It had belonged to my grandmother. I also gave her a nice sum of money to hold her until

I returned to the States to arrange for my family—mostly the Di Napoli clan of my Aunt Sophie—to take care of her.

She told me she was worried that she would not have a proper dress to be buried in and, since she could die any day, there may not be enough time for me to send her the proper dress. She explained that years ago, my grandmother had sent her a beautiful magenta velvet dress, but now that she was a widow, she could not wear it. She had to be buried in black.

I was wearing a black cotton pique dress and under it a black bra, black girdle, and black slip. I asked her if this dress would do in an emergency.

"Oh, yes," she said, beaming happily.

The priest came in, and I told him what had occurred. He blessed Raymond and me.

I went behind the curtain and changed into a dark blue tailored slack set that I had in my overnight bag. Out we went. The town was on the front lawn; when from the back of the crowd someone shouted, "Putana." [Translation: whore] Others took up the cry, and I realized then that they meant me.

The priest grasped the situation at once, and he shouted back to the crowd, "Stop! This is a good woman. She took the clothes off her back so her aunt could be buried properly."

You see, then, trousers were a man's privilege. Women in Sicily did not wear pants.

When Raymond and I returned home, Pussy asked what I had seen there. I told him the story that for a two-dollar guided tour of Palermo we saw the grave of Lucky Luciano.

"You were robbed," he said. "Charlie Lucky is buried in Queens."

No one was safe from Pussy's outrageous pranks. The more vulnerable you were, the more he put you on. Barbara, Speed Vonella's wife, was a babe in the woods, just his meat. She could never be sure if Pussy was joking or not. He spoiled many a night for her. This is just one example:

We had had a very heavy snowfall that particular night, and in walked Barbara. She asked me if Speed had arrived yet, and I told her no. Sitting at Pussy's table, she told him that Speed was late, as usual. "I guess that's how he earned his nickname." She looked very upset, so I told her that perhaps the bad weather had slowed his arrival.

Pussy gave her a look filled with mock pity. "I hate to be the one to tell you this, Barbara, but you don't deserve this kind of treatment. Speed is at the Pan American Motel with some broad."

She was uncertain whether to believe him or not, but she looked like she was about to cry. Putting all the venom I can muster into my voice, I told him, "Pussy Russo, you are wasting your time in this small town. You should be a marriage counselor in the big city."

Turning to Barbara, I told her not to pay attention to him.

"OK, don't believe me," he said, "but I made the reservation myself."

I was really annoyed with him, as he had gone too far.

"Barbara, my car has a rear engine. It will go through snow like a juggernaut. You and I will go to the Pan Am Motel. If Speed is there, I will give you a hundred dollars. If he is not there, you give me five dollars. OK?"

She believed me and continued to eat her meal. Speed never showed up that night, and Barbara went home.

The next night, Speed came in with Pussy, and I told Speed he was a mutt for making Barbara worry so. I told him that even if he had been stuck in the snow, he could have at least called her.

Pussy was laughing uncontrollably and stuttering, "T-t-tell Sp-Sp-Speed what happened."

I told him the whole story.

"You bet a hundred dollars, Frances?"

"Yes," I replied. "That's how sure I was that you were innocent."

Looking sheepishly, he mumbled something.

"What are you trying to say, Speed?"

He couldn't meet my eyes. Putting his head down, he replied, "Ah, Frances, you would have lost the bet."

I was so mad at Pussy I refused to talk to him for over a week. Speed? He kept on being Pussy's good buddy until the day Pussy died. That man was the Pied Piper.

When Raymond went on permanent day shift, I told Pussy I would look for a day job, so I could have a life with my husband.

"Okay, you can be manager of the Fish & Chips store," he said.

"What that hell are you talking about? What do I know about fish and chips?"

Speed owned eleven Fish & Chips restaurants in Monmouth and Ocean counties, and since Pussy and he were such friends, I guess he figured I could go to work there.

So Richie (that delicious Richie Vanella), Speed's brother, came in to talk to me about working for them. Annie, his wife, said, "Oh, yes, she will be good with those kids."

I was completely in the dark, and I told Richie, "What do I know about managing a Fish & Chips store?"

"Oh, we send you to a school in Ohio, and when you come back you're ready to manage a store," he said.

I went to Ohio. The Fish & Chips incident could make another book, but this is the story of the Surf, so I will not get into that.

I continued to see Pussy and talk on the phone with him. In fact, I bothered the hell out of him. We had to buy from our own distributors and so if they were short on an order (they were always short, making life miserable for all the managers), I would call him.

"Where can I buy shrimp at a reasonable price?" or "I am short of peanut oil. Where can I get it?"

With all that he had to do, he never once told me to stop bothering him with this petty stuff. God knows he had enough troubles of his own. He always came through with whatever I needed. I once apologized for bothering him so much.

"Bother me all you want, you *Sigi* bastard. I would not take a sack of gold for you."

Though they did not know it for a while, the phone in the Fish & Chips was tapped. When we found out, we thought it was because of Pussy, but dumb Barbara (dumb like a fox) hit the nail on the head. It wasn't Pussy or Speed or Richie they were monitoring; it was our respectable, legitimate partner they were investigating. Ha. Ha. He shall be nameless, but one and all know who he was.

But I digress.

Anyway, since we had nothing to hide, we talked freely on the phone. Pussy, of course, was outrageous, saying things like, "Officer, you don't mind if I talk to Frances about my sex life, do you?"

He was forever taking me out to dinner, but somehow we never got there. So, he would banter back and forth about the phone tapping, saying "I'm taking some people to the Copa Saturday. Do you want to come?"

I would say, "Well, since you're taking some people to the Copa, why not take the officer, too?"

From what happened later, I know the FBI did not take umbrage to it; rather, the officer listening was very amused. The FBI agents are human, just like everyone else.

Now about that promise to Butch that I kept for ten years to not tell anyone his real name was Fuck. I broke it only because it gave me a chance to get back at that arch prankster, Pussy, who was forever breaking my chops. It came about when Joey Agnellino took over the Surf.

Pussy was having one of his special dinners for friends and wanted everything to be perfect. "These are important men I am having tonight. No fooling around, Frances. I want only you to wait on the table," he ordered me.

I assured him that all would be exactly as he wished. I really meant for it to be so, but when the "important men" came in, one of them was Butch! I saw my golden opportunity. Whispering to Butch, "You don't know me," I seated the men at Pussy's table.

The first half hour passed without incident. I kept looking at Butch as if I were trying to place him. At one point, I asked Joey, "Don't I know him?" He informed me emphatically that I did not. Butch remained silent.

While pouring the coffee, I looked directly at Butch and blurted out, "Well, if it isn't my old friend Fuck!"

Pussy for once in his life was speechless. Not so, Joey. In a towering rage, he shouted, "Have you gone crazy? You don't know this man!"

Stone silence.

"Oh, yes, I do. Ten years ago, he came in one night wearing his five-hundred-dollar suit, his seventy-five-dollar tie, and this gorgeous shirt with a monogrammed F. I asked what the F stood for, and he told me it stands for Fuck. Ask him yourself."

All the men at the table were staring at me, as if I suddenly had gone out of my mind. Butch was scowling; he looked very menacing indeed.

"Look, if he wants to call himself Fuck, it's all right with me," I said.

Poor Pussy looked like he was going to pass out.

Flashing my most innocent smile, I continued, "Oh, I see where I have made my mistake. Since then, he has come up in the world, so now I have to call him Mr. Fuck."

This broke up Butch. Embracing me, he showered me with kisses and told Pussy, "Frannie is the best fuckin' broad in Long Branch."

This was the last time I saw Butch. I would give a great deal if I could see him again. In 1984, I heard from a mutual friend that he had been stricken with MS. I cannot picture the vibrant Butch in a wheelchair, but I know that whatever befell him, he would overcome it with courage and fortitude.

The first Christmas away from the Surf was a bad one. Everything happened at once. I took less money to be with my husband who worked days, and now that N.L. Industries had closed their plant in Sayerville, NJ, and overnight there was not only no job for Raymond, but also no unemployment. N.L. played it beautifully. It was cheaper to employ Europeans and cheaper to buy the pigment in Europe, so overnight more than 3,000 Americans were out of work. One by one, N.L. closed their plants in America. Since there was a strike the year before the plants closed (the strike lasted a year), the men were unable to collect unemployment.

The federal government had a law that stated that if anyone lost their job because of foreign employment (like moving a whole cartel to Europe) they would get some sort of settlement. Ha! No one got one dime. So, the union, the federal government, and N.L. Industries sold out these men, some who has worked for twenty or more years for them.

I have to laugh when I read about how organized crime makes the average citizen suffer because they control part of the economy, and how we the people are paying because of the drug trafficking, loan sharking, etc. Maybe so, but what about how our esteemed men in Washington, DC...senators, congressmen, presidents...working hand in glove with these criminals?

You read in the papers till today how the American people have been sold down the river by their men in government. I have more respect for the "criminal." He does not pretend to hold up the law. He is not duly sworn to uphold the law. He takes his chances. He does not hide behind a cloak of respectability, and I believe he does less damage than those arch-hypocrites. God bless America.

Again, I digress.

Anyway, that Christmas was the first time I got cash (plus a beautiful gold watch) from Pussy. When I protested that he was being more than generous, he scowled, "Listen here, kid. When a man owns a candy factory and he gives you a box of candy, he doesn't give you a goddamned thing. Now, the man who owns the factory is a busy man and the one thing that is hard for him to give you is his time, so if he gives you his time, well, now, he gave you something."

Now, I understood just how much I meant to this man. This incident will explain it further.

I was a collector of cookbooks, nothing of value, just out-of-print books and some current ones. When I first came to the Surf, I owned about seventy-five cookbooks; when I left, I had close to a thousand. I purchased about two hundred myself; the rest were gifts from the Mob.

The weekend this incident took place, Pussy had to go to Boston on "serious business" and did not intend to return till late Sunday evening.

Well, on Saturday, we were jammed as usual, and I was in the back of the cocktail lounge when I heard him call to me. There he was, in the middle of the dining room, holding up a book, and shouting, "Frances, I found it—Hershey's 1934 Cookbook."

I thanked him and told him I would rather have that book than diamond earrings. Now, when he delivered his sermon on the man who owned the candy factory, I realized that this busy man had taken the time not only to buy me a present, but also to spend a great deal of time to find something he knew I would value.

Pussy gave me many gifts over the years, but no cash. He knew that back then, I did not need the money. He also knew I was one who gave it away, mostly to worthless people, so he gave me things that I would not go out and buy for myself—jewelry, furs, expensive evening clothes. He was forever telling me, "No cash for you, Santa Claus. Who do you think you are, Pussy Russo?"

I only hope that he knew how much I loved him. I never did tell him how much he meant to me. When someone dies, it is not the things we did to that person that haunt us; it is the things we never did. Whoever said the sins of omission are the ones that hurt the most was so right.

I was at the Fish & Chips when Pussy lost his brother John, who was Pussy's idol. The sun rose and set in John, so I knew that Pussy was devastated by his sudden death.

Helen and I went to pay our respects. At the funeral parlor, Louie met us at the door. We asked how Pussy was holding up, and he told us, "He is taking it so bad he has not eaten for two days. Try to cheer him up."

Nothing we could say or do would cheer him up, but we knew how to get him to eat. He was so glad to see us, especially Helen. She had just started her bout with cancer, and he was touched that we ventured out on such a cold night (in December), traveling an hour to get there, and she so ill herself, to give whatever comfort we could. He told us this with tears in his eyes.

Helen said, "We can't stay too long, as we have not eaten yet." This was a ruse. Being the man he was, he could not let us go home hungry, so he took us for a bite and, in the process, he ate a little, too.

He said a strange thing when we returned to the funeral parlor. We walked over to the casket and looking first at John, he turned to us and said, "There goes my insurance policy."

Four months later, we understood. John was a big power in the underworld. While he lived, no one dared touch Pussy. Why Pussy was murdered, I do not know. I only know that on April 25, 1978, I lost a great friend.

A light went out of his life when John died. He was not the same man. Gone was the delightful tease; the ever-smiling man was replaced by a sad and serious one I did not know. Helen came often to see me during those final days of his life, and we discussed ways and means of cheering him up. I hit on an idea. The book always got a rise out of him, so I called him.

"Boss, I thought of a good title for my book," I chirped.

The tone in his voice told me he was responding. "Spill it, you *Sigi* bastard. I'm busy."

I continued, "I'm going to calmly call the book *Mobsters I Have Known & Loved*.

Stone silence. There is a slight chuckle on the other end of the line.

Encouraged, I gushed, "Isn't that a good title?"

"Yeah, that should sell a lot of books," he responded.

"Just think, Boss, if my book is a success, Hollywood might buy it. I will go to Hollywood."

"Yeah, you go to Hollywood, and we'll all go to jail."

Helen and I laughed till the tears rolled down our cheeks.

A week later, he called me up to ask when I thought the book would be finished. "You mean you really want me to attempt to write a book?"

"Yeah, I have no children to keep my memory alive, so when I die, you publish the book."

"Suppose I die first?"

"Then I will publish the book and give your kids the royalties."

Two months later, he was gone.

One month after Pussy's death, an FBI agent called on me. He told me that I was on the tapes of the phone tap. I told him that there was nothing I could tell him about Pussy's "alleged Mafia affiliations" and that even if I knew anything, he would be the last person I would tell.

He smiled and said, "I have been listening on and off for four years to his phone conversations. I must admit, I fell in love with the man."

I burst into tears. "You don't know the half of it."

"That's why I'm here. Tell me about him, about the days in the Surf."

For an hour or so we swapped stories. He told me of funny incidents he heard on the tapped line in Pussy's office, and I told him a little about the Surf days. As he was leaving, he turned to me and said, "Now, you can publish your book."

For years, the book lay forgotten. I never was serious about the book in the first place, and it died with Pussy, or so I thought.

After I left the Fish & Chips, Raymond and I started a small limousine business. I used to amuse my customers with Surf stories. One of my customers (who became a good friend) was Conrad Schmidt, a gentleman who worked for McGraw-Hill. He kept telling me I should write the book. I told him that I did not have any literary talent. I had bad command of English, I could not spell, and last but not least, I asked, "Who wants to read another story about the Mob?"

He told me that I should get a tape recorder and talk the story into it. I wish I had done just that; words are only black and white. They can't really convey on paper what the spoken word can offer. He seemed to think it would make a very good book. He went on to say that if the book had potential, the experts would polish it up.

I ignored him; that is, until I accidentally met him in our local Food Town Market on the tenth anniversary of Pussy's death. He greeted me with "It's been ten years now. Don't you think it's time you wrote the book?"

Over the next few weeks, I kept hearing Pussy's words, "I have no children to keep my memory alive." I started to put it down on paper, and here it is. We are told (we Catholics of Italian descent) by our grandparents, not the church, that the "dead see and hear." A nice thought. I hope it is true, because here are all the things I should have said to all those who are gone. I like to think that all my beloved dead are sitting around discussing the book.

I can hear Pussy now, "You *Sigi* bastard. You did it."

LaVergne, TN USA
28 December 2009
168198LV00003BA/34/P